A BIRD IN THE HAND

Keeping New Zealand Wildlife Safe

JANET HUNT

RANDOM HOUSE
NEW ZEALAND

For the wild ones: knowing that they are there makes all the difference

National Library of New Zealand Cataloguing-in-Publication Data
Hunt, Janet, 1951-
A bird in the hand : keeping New Zealand wildlife safe / Janet Hunt.
Includes bibliographical references.
ISBN 1-86941-563-9
1. Rare animals—New Zealand—Juvenile literature.
2. Endangered species—New Zealand—Juvenile literature.
3. Wildlife conservation—New Zealand—Juvenile literature.
I. Title.
333.9542160993—dc 21

A RANDOM HOUSE BOOK
published by
Random House New Zealand
18 Poland Road, Glenfield, Auckland, New Zealand
www.randomhouse.co.nz

First published 2003

© 2003 Janet Hunt; illustrations as listed on p. 126
The moral rights of the author have been asserted

ISBN 1 86941 563 9

Text design and layout: Janet Hunt
Cover design: Dexter Fry
Front cover photograph: Garry Norman
Back cover photographs: top, Don Merton/DOC; bottom, M.Aviss/DOC
Printed in China

Contents

Introduction *5*

1. The giant time capsule — *There ain't no moa, no moa* *8*
2. Seeking Richard Henry — *Fiordland's lost-and-found kakapo* *14*
3. A home by the river — *The story of kaki, the black stilt* *24*
4. Sharp shooter! — *Ngakeoke, or peripatus, the worm-insect* *34*
5. A liking for trees — *A home for hoiho, the yellow-eyed penguin* *38*
6. The rock group — *The very secret world of Hamilton's frog* *44*
7. Grey ghosts & shadows — *The haunting song of the South Island kokako* *50*
8. Blue blood on the mountain — *Powelliphanta, the giant snail of Taranaki* *58*
9. Walking on wrists — *Pekapeka tou poto, the short-tailed bat* *62*
10. Stoatal enemies — *Rowi, the Okarito brown kiwi* *68*
11. Oh, corker! Corker! Corker! — *Toutouwai pango, the black robin* *74*
12. When push comes to shove — *The weta with horns* *80*
13. Turf wars on Tiri — *Aroha, the one-tough takahe* *86*
14. Of holes & honey — *The riddle of hihi, the stitchbird* *94*
15. The great question — *The story of 42, the karearea or falcon* *100*
16. Bring on the clowns — *Kea and kaka, the New Zealand parrots* *106*
17. A long slow start — *A tale of a tuatara* *110*
18. All at sea — *The albatross of Taiaroa Head* *118*

References & Word List *125*

Index *128*

Macrons

Many of the common names we use for our native wildlife are taken from their Māori names — like tui, rata and weta. In Māori many of these have accents, which help to show how they are pronounced, but as they have become absorbed into the English language these accents — or macrons — are usually left off. So we have kakapo, which in Māori is kākāpō, hoiho (hōiho), takahe (takahē), pukeko (pūkeko), and so on. When a word is used as part of the English language, it has not been given a macron.

Acknowledgements

Many people have contributed to this book. They unstintingly offered enthusiasm and constructive advice, and willingly shared their considerable and specialist knowledge. My thanks particularly to: Lynn Adams, Lorrayne Alexander, Marie Alpe, Richard Anderson, Ben Barr, Paul Barrett, Merryn Bayliss, Derek Brown, Rhys Buckingham, Kate Button, Isabel Castro, Jim Clarkson, Pam Crisp, Jo Crofton, Simon Fordham, Peter Gaze, Brian Gill, Ian Gill, Diane Gleeson, Andy Grant, Peter Griffen, Noel Hyde, Andrew Jeffs, Susan Keall, John Kendrick, Sarah King, Bruce Knight, Mary Lewis, Brian Lloyd, Leigh Marshall, Liz Mellish, Don Merton, Ferne McKenzie, Colin Miskelly, Janice Molloy, Greg Moorcroft, Nicola Patrick, Anna Petersen, Deb Price, Emily Sancha, Alan Saunders, Debbie Stewart, Robert Stone, Noelene Taylor, Shirley Thornbury, Paul van Klink, Kath Walker, Barbara Walter, Ray Walter, Chris Ward, Bryan Welch and Karen Wells.

My appreciation also to my editor, Jenny Hellen; the team at Random House New Zealand; the DOC Image Librarian, Ferne McKenzie, and the staff and students of Te Huruhi School.

Always, my love and thanks to my family and friends, especially Elwyn Hunt. And last, because most, my love and thanks to chief critic, Peter Haines.

Introduction

I AM HAUNTED by a grainy black-and-white photograph. It was taken at North-East Harbour on Campbell Island in 1888. Three men pose beside a whaling boat on a grey shore. It is probably summer but it looks bitterly cold. Campbell is the most southerly of New Zealand's subantarctic islands and lies at 52º 35' south, 169º 10' east. The men are wearing workmen's clothes — caps, thick woollen trousers, jackets and heavy boots.

One of the men is sitting uncomfortably on a rock. He is holding a rifle with its long barrel pointing skyward. A second man sits on another rock behind him, his face almost hidden. It's the closest man, the one on the left of the picture, who catches my eye, because he is holding two live royal albatross, one in each arm like children or big teddy bears. They are huge and beautiful and outlined in snowy-white against his dark clothes. They don't seem concerned. The one on the right looks at the ground as if puzzled to find itself in this situation. At first glance, its large webbed feet appear splayed as if it expects at any moment to walk or swim or take to the air, but

Alien animals

Maori imported kiore, a small bush rat, and dogs. Europeans brought cats, dogs, rabbits, possums, stoats, weasels, ferrets, mice, two more kinds of rat, hedgehogs, pigs, goats, deer, sheep and cows. Some of them eat the same food as the native wildlife, and others eat the wildlife itself.

From top — some of the introduced animals: a mouse eating kiekie fruit; a weasel about to have an eggy feast; a hedgehog; a stoat and a ship rat eating fantail chicks at the nest.

if you look closer you can see that they are tied. It is unlikely that either bird will walk or swim or fly again. The title of the photograph is 'Albatross Hunter'.

The story of New Zealand wildlife since the arrival of humans is often brutal and shocking. It starts with Maori migration and settlement about 800 years ago. They were followed about 500 years later by Europeans. They poured in and shaped this new land to suit themselves.

Just like the albatross hunters, it must have seemed to pioneers of both races that the land, waters and skies were exploding with birds, sea creatures and fish that were theirs for the taking, and that it would always be that way.

Wrong!

Directly and indirectly, wild creatures on the three main islands and on many offshore islands were stalked, ambushed, hunted, eaten, burned, turned out of their homes and starved. Their living places were destroyed by flame and axe and they were killed by humans and by the animals and diseases that came with them.

The casualties were enormous. Thirty-four species of bird became extinct in pre-European times, and another 16 after Europeans arrived. Amphibians, fish, reptiles, one bat and countless invertebrates also disappeared forever.

But it's not all bad news. We have lost a lot but we have to count our blessings. New Zealand has over 700 islands and though many were invaded by people and introduced animals, not all of them suffered as much as the biggest ones. Some were like castles with moats to keep out invaders. Wild creatures remained safe in remote and inaccessible sea-ringed places. We would have lost even more if we had not had those island fortresses.

And islands continue to be a very important part of the New Zealand wildlife story. Some have been major sanctuaries for a long time and others are now becoming safer as all introduced animals are removed. Once they are safe, they can be used as temporary homes for endangered creatures and although some of those endangered creatures may never again live on the main islands, others have already returned, some to places where they have been gone for over a hundred years.

There is a new kind of island as well. These islands are not surrounded by water but by rings of steel, by fences and trap lines to stop predators and competitors in their tracks. Many are just like real island fortresses, and more secure than any castle. Some are even in the hearts of big cities.

There are other excellent things happening. Some species, thought to be extinct, have been found. And a great number of enthusiastic, energetic and dedicated people are working very hard on behalf of wildlife. They are making safe places, planting and fencing bush, looking after streams and rivers, giving their land legal protection, learning how to trap predators and being responsible animal owners. Others are working with the wildlife itself, breeding and rescuing endangered creatures, learning more and more ways to help make them safe.

A Bird in the Hand tells the stories of some of the stars of the wildlife stage. They are plump, cuddly, cute and colourful and have amazing personalities. It also tells of some creatures that are less well-known: they are slimy and furtive and one at least has disgusting table manners, but they are no less interesting or important. Almost all are hanging on by a claw or a feather and with a lot of help.

Their stories are similar to the stories of all New Zealand wildlife, including the many species that had to be left out. They too are there in the bush, on the coast, islands and mountain tops. Many are endangered. They are not hard to find out about, and more and more you can see them in their special places — island sanctuaries such as Tiritiri Matangi, Kapiti and Matiu/Somes, or in the many mainland islands, reserves and zoos.

New Zealand wildlife is diverse, it is extraordinary, it is weird and wacky and wonderful. Above all, it is found nowhere else on Earth.

A Bird in the Hand is about caring for what you have. The traditional proverb was: A bird in the hand is worth two in the bush. It meant you should care for what you have and not long for something else. The proverb for today is: A bird in the hand *means* two in the bush. It means that if we care for what we have, we may one day have more.

Who is DOC?

Is DOC a man? Is DOC a woman? No, DOC is lots of men and women. DOC is like a person who appears in all sorts of places and times to help save the wild creatures of New Zealand. 'DOC' stands for the Department of Conservation *Te Papa Atawhai*, the part of the government that looks after wild animals and the places where they live. DOC was formed in 1987. Before that, it was the job of the Wildlife Service to care for New Zealand's wild animals. DOC is a main character in this book.

The predator-proof fence at the Karori Wildlife Sanctuary in Wellington — this is an island in a city.

1 The giant time capsule
There ain't no moa, no moa

*No moa, no moa
In old Ao-tea-roa
Can't get 'em
They've et 'em
They're gone and there ain't no moa.*

— W. Chamberlain
New Zealand song

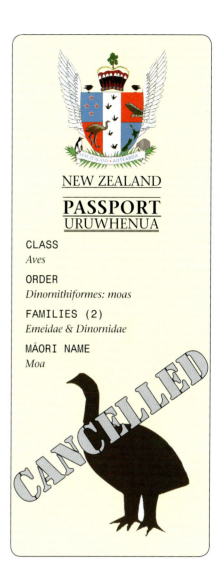

WHEN MAORI FIRST pulled canoes onto the shores of New Zealand about 800 years ago, they stepped into a giant time capsule. For around 80 million years the islands of New Zealand had been on their own in the middle of the ocean. During those millions of years, the plants, birds and other living creatures on these islands had evolved differently from any others on Earth.

It was an astonishing, giant-filled country. There were not only enormous birds but also huge snails, weta and primitive animals with ancient family trees, whose ancestors had been alive with the dinosaurs. It must have seemed a land of great wonder and plenty even though it lacked the fruit and vegetables that Maori knew in the Pacific — a bit like walking through the doors of a giant supermarket, in fact!

Many of those creatures no longer exist, but even today New Zealand has more unique plants and animals than any other country in the world.

To understand why this is, we must go to the beginning of time, about 4,000,000,000 years ago. There was no sea and planet Earth was a sizzling, spinning ball of molten rock — can you imagine how hot it has to be to make a rock melt?

There was no air to breathe and no water to drink. There were no living things at all in that world of whirling, swirling dust and gas.

It took a long time, maybe 100 million years, but slowly the earth cooled. A crust formed on the outside and gases began to make an atmosphere.

And then it started to rain. It poured, not just for a day or a month but for millions of years. Slowly the rain filled the hollows of the earth and the world's oceans were formed. Still, the earth was not at all like it is today.

All the Earth's land was in one piece — the vast supercontinent

Our planet — like a giant Jaffa

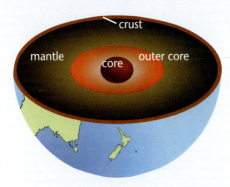

The land we stand on is the earth's *crust*. The core in the middle is as hot and molten as it was in the beginning of earth-time thousands of millions of years ago. Between the crust and the hot part there's a layer called the *mantle*. This layer is neither hard and cold like the crust nor molten and hot like the core but somewhere in the middle. We can't see or feel it happening, but the crust is floating on top of the mantle like a cork on water.

As it floats, parts of the crust rub and push and slide against one another. Sometimes they move suddenly, jerking and graunching and causing earthquakes. Sometimes the crust splits apart and hot stuff from inside spills out to make volcanoes. Sometimes the parts of the crust collide and push against each other until they rear up thousands of metres above sea level to make mountain ranges like the Southern Alps and the Himalayas.

The land we call New Zealand is on the edge of one of the floating pieces of crust. It has moved around so much that about 570 million years ago it was in the *Northern* Hemisphere, but 250 million years later it was almost as far south as the Antarctic! It has been *tropical* and it has been covered in *ice*, and several times it has been submerged beneath the ocean.

of Pangaea. For a very long time no one knew it had existed, but in 1858 a man called Antoine Snider noticed that if you cut up a map of the world's land masses, you could push the pieces together like a jigsaw puzzle. People laughed. 'What a fool!' they said. 'How stupid can you be?' They soon forgot about it, but good ideas don't go away and 54 years later another man, Alfred Wegener, reached the same conclusion. It was Wegener who named the supercontinent *Pangaea*, which means 'all earth'.

'Poppycock!' people said again, and added some ruder things as well. 'It's just not possible! And anyway, if that's true, how come this so-called *Pangaea* isn't still here? How can land move around? It's not floating!'

Little did they know. By 1948 scientists had realised that Snider and Wegener were correct. The land we live on really is 'floating', though it takes millions of years to go even a tiny distance.

Pangaea has been gone a long time. First, around 180 million years ago, it split in two and formed a northern continent called *Laurasia* and a southern continent called *Gondwana*.

Later, Laurasia and Gondwana also broke up. Laurasia became the land masses we call North America, Europe and most of Asia. Gondwana drifted south and broke apart to become South America, Africa, India, Antarctica, Australia and, of course, New Zealand. Remember, this took millions and millions of years to happen.

New Zealand did not float away from Gondwana until around 86 million years ago. At that time reptiles, including the dinosaurs, were still bosses of the earth. So it was a selection of those reptiles or their descendants, including amphibians, the first birds and a host of smaller animals such as insects, snails and worms, that were left high and dry on New Zealand's shores. Apart from short-tailed bats, there were not yet any mammals.

But then, suddenly, 65 million years ago, everything changed. The age of reptiles ended. Almost overnight, dinosaurs disappeared and were replaced by a new order. Cloven-hoofed, warm-blooded, grass-munching mammals grazed swamps and roamed prairies with pointy-toothed, meat-eating mammals on their heels; long-armed mammals swung through treetops and blubber-covered mammals cavorted in the seas. There were mammals as big as mammoths and mammals as small as mice; they made homes near the icy poles and found ways to live in the hottest tropics. Humans are mammals. Mammals were everywhere, except . . .

Bats aside, there were still none in New Zealand, where the reptiles, birds, fish, insects and other invertebrates just carried on by themselves, making up their own rules. Like the mammals elsewhere, they evolved together, each with its own special food, its unique habitat or living space and its unique way of breeding. Many echoed mammals elsewhere in the way they lived and behaved — like the tiny wren that lived in rocks and ran around like a mouse. Some became giants and a great number of the birds gave up flying for comfortable lives on the ground. And that included the moa.

Alas for moa, they had no wings whatsoever — not even itty-bitty useless ones. Even if they had been able to fly, they would not have been saved. They were just too big and easy to catch.

That must have been what the first Maori thought. Because the climate and vegetation in New Zealand were different from what they were used to in the Pacific, hunting and fishing were very important. We know from bones in old campsites and places where Maori lived that the moa was a popular meal, along with a number of other birds. Moa were most likely snared or hunted with dogs and killed with spears, although they could give a mighty kick — maybe there's good reason for the 'terrible' that's part of their scientific name.

It is said that a Maori named Apa came across a moa on the side of Putauaki (Mt Edgecumbe). He thought it was some kind of strange man. He struck a blow at the leg it was standing on, and it kicked him so violently with the drawn-up leg that he was hurled over a cliff and killed.

The last moa died around the year 1500, about 500 years ago. There is a Maori saying, *Ka ngaro i te ngaro a te moa*, which records that passing. It means 'lost as the moa is lost'.

Mammals

Mammals are a particular kind of animal. They have warm blood which makes them very adaptable and able to live in a lot of climates. They are born alive (not hatched from eggs) and their mothers feed them on milk when they are young. They have hair to keep them warm. Like birds, mammals long ago also descended from reptiles.

Some mammals like milk all their lives.

Ratites

Moa belong to the group of flightless birds known as *ratites*. They are running birds with powerful legs and a flat breastbone. Kiwi, emu, cassowary, ostrich and rhea are also ratites.

Moa not only had no wings, their feathers were downy and fur-like and no use for flying. Although some feathers have been found, we don't know what colours these birds might have been.

This baggy sort of moa is based on a rock drawing made by moa hunters in a South Canterbury cave over 500 years ago.

Moa facts

- There were 11 different species of moa in two groups. The first group, the family Emeidae, were stout with short strong legs. They had very descriptive names such as 'little bush moa', 'upland moa', 'heavy-footed moa', 'crested moa', 'Mappin's moa', 'eastern moa', 'stout-legged moa' and 'coastal moa'. Coastal moa, *Eurapteryx geratnoides*, was probably the smallest, at around one metre high. The most massive was the heavy-footed moa, with the excellent scientific name *Pachyornis elephantopus*. It weighed around 240 kg but was only about 1.8 metres tall — to the top of its head!

- The other group, the family Dinornithidae, had longer leg bones, were generally taller and would have won all the running races. There were only three species in this group: the slender bush moa, the large bush moa and the tallest bird ever known, the famous giant moa, *Dinornis giganteus*. 'Dinornis' means 'terrible bird', in the same way as 'dinosaur' means 'terrible lizard'. *D. giganteus* was over 3 metres tall, some say up to 4 metres — which means the top of its head when it was standing erect was higher than a netball hoop or the crossbar on a rugby goal. *D. giganteus* also weighed around 240 kg — twice the weight of Jonah Lomu — and its egg was around 4 kg. *That's one big chicken! That's one heck of an omelette!*

An artist's impression of the Maori camp on the Dart River in Fiordland about 400 years ago. Women are preparing ti stems for baking and men are preparing freshly-skinned moa leg joints. This site was used as long ago as 1250AD as a place for making stone tools.

Taxonomy — the science of names

Taxonomy is the science of sorting out or classifying living things according to how closely related they are. A *taxonomist* is the scientist who makes those decisions. It's like making a family tree.

A *species* is a group of organisms that normally interbreed in nature. So although kaka and kea are parrots and look very similar they are considered separate species because they do not interbreed in the wild.

A number of very closely related species are put together in a group called a *genus*. So kaka and kea belong to the same genus, *Nestor*.

Each organism has a two-part name. The first part is their genus name and the second is their species name. The scientific name is always written in italics. The genus name has a capital letter but the species name does not.

So kaka are *Nestor meridionalis* and kea are *Nestor notabilis*. There are also sometimes *sub*-species and that means a third name is added — so the North Island kaka is *Nestor meridionalis septentrionalis* and the South Island kaka is *Nestor meridionalis meridionalis*.

Sometimes, if the genus has been already mentioned, it is shortened to just its first letter the next time it is mentioned. So you might write *N. notabilis* the second time you used the kea's scientific name.

Scientists estimate that there are at least 3 million, but perhaps as many as 30 million living species. That takes a lot of organising! So after species and genera (more than one genus), more groups are made, each bigger than the one before.

Genera are grouped into *families*; families are grouped into *orders*; orders are grouped into *classes*; classes are grouped into *phyla*; and phyla are grouped into the biggest group of all, *kingdoms*.

Any one of these groups, from species to kingdom, is called a *taxon*. Several groups make a *taxa*.

Of course, this is a very simplified explanation. Taxonomy is a complicated science. Once it was based on things like physical and behavioural similarities but in the 21st century it uses extra information, including DNA and genetic analysis, to help make groupings.

That is why hihi (see Chapter 14), that were thought to belong to the family Melphagidae or honey-eaters, are now thought to be something else. They look quite a lot like other honey-eaters — and eat honey — but are genetically different.

RIP: Extinct birds of New Zealand

Another of New Zealand's giant birds, the giant eagle, *Harpagornis moorei*, disappeared about the same time as the moa, perhaps because the moa was its main food. It was the largest eagle ever known, with wings that were 3 metres from tip to tip and a weight of up to 13 kg. If you'd spotted *H. moorei* coming after you through the trees, you'd have thought it was truly terrible!

You can read more about extinct birds at www.kcc.org.nz/birds/extinct/list.htm

2 Seeking Richard Henry
Fiordland's lost-and-found kakapo

There are two Richard Henrys in the story of the kakapo.
One is a man, the other is a bird.

(I) Richard Henry, kakapo

THE KAKAPO LIVED ON A SHELF on the south wall of an area known as the Gulliver, 900 metres above a rocky Fiordland valley. Steep cliffs plunged to the valley floor below and high bluffs towered above. He knew every millimetre of his mountain kingdom. He had been there on his own for a long, long time. He didn't mind. Parrots don't think about these things.

The shelf was 300 metres wide and about one and a half kilometres long, and was covered in small trees, scrubby bushes and low-growing mountain plants. The kakapo spent all of every day asleep and every night he browsed on leaves and twigs.

Once a year, he tidied his track-and-bowl system and, out of habit, did a bit of booming. (Read about tracks, bowls and booming on p. 22.) Sometimes, in the distance across the mountains, he heard the answering *whoomph* of other kakapo and would send a *whoomph* back, but he never saw or expected to see them.

Then one day, his sleep was disturbed by the *thudthudthud* of an enormous grey flying thing. Deep within, a memory stirred of the giant eagles that had once hunted his ancestors. He froze. The grey thing landed on the shelf, and strange creatures like featherless birds appeared. He didn't like this one bit. Very slowly and quietly, he melted into the bushes and hid.

His strategy was to lie low so that when the birds had what they wanted, they would go and leave him in peace. But only the *thudthud* thing flew away and the featherless birds stayed behind. They made a nest out of what looked like large flapping leaves. That night, he could hear their strange loud calls. They made a lot of noise. They carried extra small bright eyes. Everything about them signalled danger. He knew he must keep clear.

But that was not easy because they were everywhere. Each day the kakapo had to find a new hiding place and at night he didn't get much to eat because the featherless birds were still about.

Sometimes they came very close and he held his breath and closed his eyes. He looked like a piece of moss and the featherless birds did not see him.

Then the *thudthud* thing returned. This time, as well as more featherless birds, there was a dog. The kakapo had seen dogs once

NEW ZEALAND
PASSPORT
URUWHENUA

CLASS
Aves

ORDER
Pstittaciformes: cockatoos & parrots

FAMILY
Psittacidae: parrots
Kakapo has its own subfamily, *Strigopinae*

SCIENTIFIC NAME
Strigops habroptilus. It is the only species in this genus.

COMMON NAME
Ground parrot, owl parrot, night parrot

MĀORI NAME
Kākāpō, tarapō, tarepō

Richard Henry, star kakapo

The kakapo named Richard Henry has never been easy to catch. On Maud Island, when he needed a health check, he was taken to a holding pen where he lay on his side pretending to be dead. Then he very slowly got to his feet, snuck into the cover of kawakawa seedlings, and took off!

He did a similar thing on Hauturu (Little Barrier) when he was chosen to be filmed with David Attenborough for the BBC's *Living Planet* series. He was supposed to show how kakapo will freeze when they are approached. Not Richard Henry — he wanted to do another slow-motion sneak right off the set!

Don Merton holding Richard Henry on Te Hoiere (Maud Island) in 1999.

before and knew he was in serious trouble. A dog can kill a kakapo in seconds.

He heard it coming. It made horrible snuffling, panting noises. It could smell him. He panicked and ran towards the cliff. Maybe he could hide there, or if he needed to, he could jump — though it was a long way down.

Too late! One of the featherless birds was blocking his way and another was behind with the dog. He turned, spreading his wings, knowing it was hopeless, and raised his foot to strike. He would fight to the death! But the featherless bird was quick. It swooped and grabbed him, pinning his wings, holding his legs.

'Gotcha!' said a voice. 'Richard Henry kakapo!'

By 1950 the Wildlife Service of the Department of Internal Affairs was worried. No one had heard or seen a kakapo for a long time. Did they still exist, or had they joined the moa and great eagle on New Zealand's list of extinct birds?

The Wildlife Service started looking. A number of expeditions through the 1950s found nothing, but then, in March 1958, a search party found freshly chewed leaves and kakapo feathers in an isolated valley of Fiordland.

This was good news. But how many birds were there? How did they live? Were they breeding? The Wildlife Service knew almost nothing about these night-prowling, ground-dwelling creatures. How could they find out?

Kakapo were still alive in Fiordland only because it was such hard country. Searchers had to lug heavy packs through steep valleys and up high peaks. There could be 500 mm of rain in a night, and lashing, battering wind, and cold so intense that two sleeping bags were not enough. On the rare days when the sun shone, sandflies came out in their thousands, biting bare skin and getting into eyes, noses, ears and food. And the birds were stubbornly secretive. They did not want to be found.

It was hard, hard work but in the end, five male kakapo were captured and taken to aviaries at the Mount Bruce National Wildlife Centre in the Wairarapa. One by one, while their carers watched helplessly, they died. Not enough was known about how they lived and ate to keep them alive. It was very disheartening.

Twenty years passed. In 1974 searching resumed but it was much easier, with helicopters to carry men and materials into the hills.

Eighteen birds were captured in Fiordland. This time they were set free on a safe island, Te Hoiere (Maud Island) in the Marlborough Sounds. Again, they were all males. As far as anyone knew, these kakapo were the only ones left. With no prospect of breeding, they were technically extinct.

But that was not so. Soon after, a small population of about 200 kakapo was found on Stewart Island, where there were wild cats, but no stoats. But time was running out. Almost as the Wildlife Service watched, the Stewart Island kakapo were disappearing as well! The wild cats were killing and eating them. They had to be moved. Forty-two males and 19 females were taken to safety on other islands. Eventually it became clear that the best place of all was an island called Whenua Hou (Codfish Island).

Whenua Hou is three kilometres off the west coast of Stewart Island. The seas are wild, it is isolated and the weather is terrible. There are no roads, and the best way to get there is by helicopter. However, there are 1400 hectares of kakapo-friendly bush, and no stoats, possums or rats. In particular, the island has rimu forest which provides good food for growing chicks. Three DOC staff work there.

In 2002 there was a good rimu-fruiting season. With the help of DOC staff and more than 100 volunteers, 23 chicks were hatched and fledged, and kakapo numbers shot up to 86. It has taken a long time and there is still a lot to learn, but it seems that humans at last know how to help this amazing bird survive.

Richard Henry is the only kakapo survivor from mainland New Zealand. He is adaptable, wily and placid, and has had a long and interesting life.

After he was captured in 1975 he was flown to Te Hoiere, but in the 1980s it became unsafe after stoats swam there from the mainland. And so, in 1982, Richard Henry and the three other kakapo on the island were sent to Hauturu (Little Barrier) in the Hauraki Gulf.

Richard Henry lived there for 14 years. But Hauturu is so mountainous that it was hard for DOC to manage the kakapo. They could just disappear into the trees and no one would know if they were dead or alive. Some were not seen for years at a time.

In the 1990s the kakapo were taken off Hauturu and Richard Henry was returned to Te Hoiere. Traps on the island now make sure that any stoats that turn up are soon killed. In 1998 he mated with Flossie, a female kakapo from Stewart Island, and fathered three

April, 1982. This kakapo was killed by a wild cat at Saddle Creek on Stewart Island.

Superstars

Kakapo are superstars! People fall in love with their owl-parrot faces, their soft green feathers, their exotic perfume and their quirky, determined personalities.

Why else would so many people spend so much time and so much money — $1,000,000 per year in recent years — to save them? Because they stand for all that is beautiful and precious about the New Zealand bush and the creatures still living within its leafy walls.

The kakapo recovery team

Many people have dedicated years to saving the kakapo — people like Don Merton, Operations Officer of the National Kakapo Team. In 1960, as a trainee with the Wildlife Service, he was involved in some of the first searches in Fiordland. Since then he has been there every step of the way. He is now a world authority on the management and recovery of threatened species. Don has not been alone. Hundreds of people have given months and years to saving the kakapo. Even in the worst conditions and when it seemed all hope was lost, they kept going. It has been a great team effort.

Don is on the left in this photograph of volunteers and DOC staff who were involved in round-the-clock monitoring of kakapo nests on Whenua Hou in 2002. More than 100 volunteers helped.

chicks: two males named 'Gulliver' and 'Sinbad' after the area of Fiordland where he was found, and a female named 'Kuia' after the local iwi, Ngati Kuia.

The 2002 kakapo breeding season was such a great success that suddenly the kakapo recovery team had an unexpected but pleasant problem — not enough space!

A new safe home was prepared on Te Kakahu (Chalky Island) in Fiordland. Stoats were eradicated and permanent traps set the same as on Te Hoiere. Any stoat that lands will soon be caught. On 7 July 2002 Richard Henry and nine females (Fuchsia, Hoki, Jane, Kuia, Sandra, Sara, Solstice, Wendy and Zephyr) and four other males (Gumboots, Piripi, Smoko and Whiskas) were moved there. DOC staff hope Richard Henry will father even more chicks.

As he was clearly an aged adult when he was captured in 1975, Richard Henry is *at least* 40 years old. However, Dr Mick Clout, a Professor of Ecology at the University of Auckland, points out that Richard Henry may have been among the last kakapo chicks ever hatched in Fiordland after stoats arrived there in the 1890s. That would make Richard Henry kakapo close to 100! *Time for a letter from the Queen.*

The winter camp of the kakapo expedition in the Sinbad Gully, July 1975. You can see how steep the mountains are and how cold it was!

Inset: The kakapo 'Jill' is held by Chris Smuts-Kennedy while John Cheyne, dog Mandy and Don Merton look on. 'Jill' turned out to be a male. 'She' was the second kakapo caught in the Esperance Valley, in 1974.

Richard Henry outside his boatshed on Pigeon Island, March 1900.

Museums paid very well for specimens. When Richard Henry first began to hunt birds to send overseas, he found plenty to take, including kakapo. Charles Douglas, the explorer, wrote in the 1860s that he had seen kakapo shaken out of trees like apples! That was soon to change — and all because of the rabbit.

(II) Richard Henry, man

Richard Henry was 30 when he came to New Zealand in the 1870s. He was an observant and curious person and he loved nature. He mostly worked on farms in the lower South Island but some of the time he was a hunter and bird-collector, killing native birds for skins and even catching live birds to send to museums around the world.

In the late 1870s there was a crisis on the farms that changed everything — for Richard Henry and for New Zealand. Rabbits had been brought here in the late 1830s for sport, for food and to remind homesick settlers of the British Isles. But there were no natural rabbit enemies and before long there was a sea of brown, hopping, nibbling bodies. They had eaten all the farmers' pastures and their profits.

'Why don't we get something to eat the rabbits?' people asked. 'We know!' they said. 'Let's get ferrets, stoats and weasels!'

Some people said, 'No!' They said the ferrets, stoats and weasels would be a greater evil than the rabbits.

And they were right. The ferrets, stoats and weasels ate *some* rabbits but they also ate birds, eggs and other native animals.

The birds began to disappear in front of Richard Henry's eyes. Others saw what was happening too, and asked the government to make some places where New Zealand wildlife would be safe. So in 1894 three islands were purchased — Hauturu, in the Hauraki Gulf; Kapiti, off the south-west coast of the North Island, and Resolution in Fiordland.

In July 1894 Richard Henry became the caretaker of Resolution and set up camp on a small next-door island, Pigeon Island. For more than ten years he and his dog and a young helper rowed and sailed the unfriendly waters of the fiords to take hundreds of endangered birds, including kakapo and kiwi, from the mainland to Resolution.

Sadly, all Richard Henry's work was for nothing. Stoats are good swimmers and they soon crossed the 900 m from the mainland to Resolution. Imagine how Richard Henry felt in August 1900 when he wrote, 'I am very sorry to have to say that I saw a weasel on Resolution . . . quite a little thing, no bigger than a rat & nearly white in colour. It was tracking something among the broken rocks on the shore . . .' He tried to stop the invaders, but it was no use. The birds he loved were doomed.

In 1908 Richard Henry moved to Kapiti, where he worked as caretaker for two years. He died in Helensville on 13 November, 1929. The only person at his funeral was the Helensville postmaster.

I spy

Kakapo-saving equipment is now state-of-the-art. All kakapo wear little harnesses with radio transmitters on their backs. The transmitters send a signal that searchers detect with special receivers and aerials. It's a lot easier than in the early days of kakapo rescue when searchers had to walk miles and *still* couldn't find the birds.

Even better, the kakapo team have developed a device called the *Snark*, after the mythical beast in the Lewis Carroll poem 'The hunting of the Snark'. A Snark is a little box with a radio receiver, a data logger and special computer software. It is placed in the bush so that when a transmitter-wearing kakapo goes by in the night, the information is recorded. Staff simply come by the next day and read the information from the Snark onto portable mini-computers. *What would Richard Henry the man think of that?*

Because nesting time is crucial, nothing happens in the nest that people don't know about. A small infra-red camera records everything on video around the clock. Every night, in a tent nearby, minders watch a monitor connected to the camera. When the female kakapo leaves her eggs to feed, a small electric blanket is lowered over the eggs to keep them warm until she returns. When she comes back, it disappears. She knows nothing!

If minders see a predator on the screen, they push a panic button which triggers a bang, flash and puff of smoke to frighten it away. *Magic!*

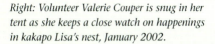

Miniature infra-red camera used at nest sites to record all activities, Whenua Hou, May 1997.

Right: Volunteer Valerie Couper is snug in her tent as she keeps a close watch on happenings in kakapo Lisa's nest, January 2002.

Right: Sandra King and kakapo dog, Heidi, are radio-tracking kakapo on Whenua Hou, August 1995.

Breeding kakapo

The ideal thing is for kakapo to raise their chicks in the wild, but sometimes a more active helping hand is needed.

Kakapo 'A2' hatching at the takahe breeding unit at Burwood Bush, Te Anau, March 1999.

Daryl Eason is caring for Gromete, an underweight kakapo chick, March 1997.

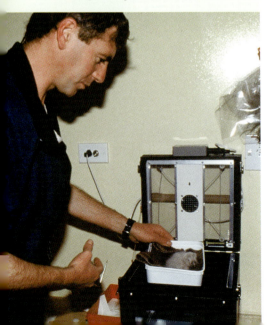

SCRARK! — BOOM! — CHING!
—the complicated sex life of the kakapo

Boom! Boom! Kakapo mating is a noisy business. Kakapo are *lek* breeders, which means that when the time is right for breeding, male kakapo gather to make a racket and brag and strut in order to attract females.

Chicks need protein to grow and the best protein for kakapo comes from trees such as the rimu pictured above. So breeding only happens when the rimu or some other plant that produces a super-duper crop (or *mast*) every few years is going to have a lot of fruit and kakapo know it will be a good year to breed and get ready to . . . BOOM!

It happens on a high point, a hill or a ridge. First, there's scrapping and scrarking over the best spot, then each male creates a *court*. He makes a number of kakapo-sized bowls in the ground and joins them up with a system of trimmed and tidy pathways. Often the bowls are near trees or rocks, which make good amplifiers. A collection of several kakapo courts is called an *arena* or *lek*.

The male kakapo takes deeper and deeper breaths until his chest is pumped as tight as a feathered football. Then he lowers himself into a bowl and makes deep grunting sounds. WHOOMPH! WHOOMPH! The sound, like the bass thump of a stereo, can be heard up to five kilometres away. He may make up to a thousand booms an hour for hours on end, every night for up to three months. *Call noise control!*

When a female kakapo hears the booms, she comes to find the best male to father her chicks. Once he realises there is a female in the area, the male's calls change to a higher *ching* sound to draw her to him.

In 1975, technological advances enabled Don Merton and his team to see the kakapo's nocturnal courtship display for the first time. Using a 'light intensifier' scope which enabled them to see in the dark, they watched what happens. As well as booming and chinging, the male slowly walks backwards with his handsome wings outstretched, gently waving them up and down, clicking his bill and rocking from side to side. If the female fancies him, they mate and she returns to her area to make a nest, lay eggs and raise the chicks by herself.

She nests in a hole 60 cm wide by 30 cm high, among the rocks or tree roots. She lays from two to four eggs, which take 30 days to hatch. Young kakapo are fledged at 11 to 12 weeks and on their own after eight to 10 months.

Females are not the only ones attracted by booming. Young male kakapo go along to admire from the sidelines and dream about the night when it's their turn to crank up the volume.

Kakapo facts

The scientific name for kakapo is *Strigops habroptilus*. This means 'owl-face, soft-feathered'. Kakapo have also been called 'owl-parrots' because they have an owl-like facial disc. Among the things that make them parrots, are their hooked beaks and two-toes forward, two-toes backward feet. The Maori name, 'kākāpō', means 'night parrot'.

- Kakapo live alone, roosting by day and foraging for food after dark. They can travel many kilometres in a single night.

- They are strictly vegetarian. They eat a wide variety of trees and plants, and happily switch to unfamiliar foods — like apples — when they need to. Because of all those vegetables and all that fibre, *kakapoos* are quite recognisable. They have a distinctive 'coiled spaghetti' structure.

- Kakapo have short, cat-like whiskers which probably help them to get around at night without bumping into things. Kakapo chicks not only have whiskers, they purr when they are expecting to be fed! They chatter and gossip a great deal to each other in the nest.

- They have super-soft, yellow-green feathers which are excellent camouflage. When kakapo are startled they freeze, which, in combination with their colour, makes them extremely difficult to see. That is why searchers have sometimes felt like they were *chasing green shadows*.

- Kakapo have a sweet, slightly musty scent, which is said to be quite pleasant. It is similar to the smell of one of the bushes kakapo like to eat, *Alseuosmia banksii*. Unfortunately it is a dead giveaway for keen-nosed hunters like stoats, rats and cats.

- Instead of flying, kakapo *climb*. They use their beaks and strong legs to go up trees and use their short wings a bit like parachutes — to break the fall when they descend suddenly. Sometimes rather clumsily!

- Kakapo are the heaviest parrots in the world. Males weigh from 2 to 4 kg, females a little less at 1 to 2 kg. Males have wider faces and their wing feathers are patterned right to the end and down both sides of the vane. The females' feathers have a plain edge on one side and on the tip.

Find out more about kakapo at www.kakaporecovery.org.nz; www.doc.govt.nz; www.kcc.org.nz

Kakapo Suzanne and her foster chicks, W1 (45 days old) and W2 (52 days old), April 2002.

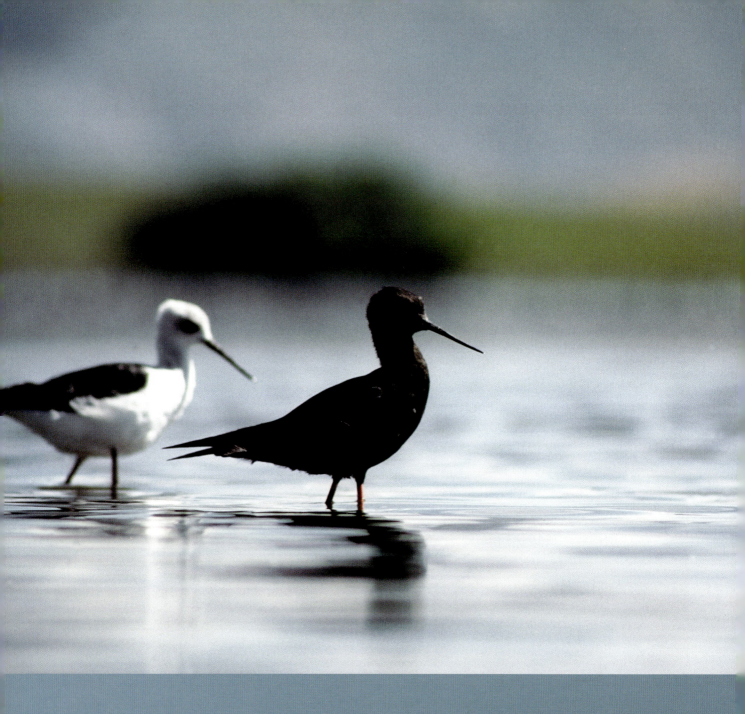

3 A home by the river

The story of kaki, the black stilt

MRS BONES NEVER had the pleasure of flying high or wading down a river, but she was a very important bird. By the time she died, she had many grandchildren, great-grandchildren, and even great-great-grandchildren. She lived at the Kaki Captive Breeding Centre at Twizel in the middle of the Upper Waitaki River basin, high in the mountains of the South Island.

Mrs Bones was hatched from an egg taken from a wild nest in 1990 and hand-reared at the centre. She was a cute chick, covered in speckled-brown fluff that was replaced by black and white feathers as she grew. By the time she was two years old the white feathers had moulted and she was completely black. She was an adult.

Instead of being set free at nine months old, she had been selected to become a breeding bird. She was paired up with a handsome male named Mr Bones. It was a good match. For 10 years they lived in the aviary together, and between them they produced many fertile eggs.

The aviary is 15 metres square, with water running through it, and has little islands and tussock. It is very natural and very nice, but of course it does have netting around it. Mrs Bones had never known anything else, but she had also never forgotten what every kaki knows: that danger comes from above.

One day in the year 2000, she was pottering in the stream, not far from Mr Bones. The sky was blue and the day was warm. It was very pleasant and peaceful.

Suddenly, a shadow fell across the water and a dark shape blotted the sun. It was a harrier hawk, high above the aviary! His bold, fierce eye was looking straight at her!

Although she was safe, Mrs Bones was terrified. She panicked. She cried out and flew up, up, faster and faster, until *WHAM!* She hit the netting, catching her beak in the mesh. No one saw her fall, her beak broken and hanging uselessly.

But the staff soon found her. They knew she would die without help. There are five bones in a kaki beak, three in the top and two in the bottom, and all of them had snapped. Tiny, precise instruments would be needed to fix them. There was nothing in Twizel.

They phoned Mark Colson, the nearest veterinarian, in the town of Geraldine, 150 kilometres and one and a half hours' drive away. 'Bring her over,' he said. 'I'll call John and we'll see what we can do.' He phoned John Jensen, the local dentist. 'I've got a special patient for you,' he said. 'It's urgent!'

Mark anaesthetised Mrs Bones and John carefully glued a tiny splint on each side of her bill, using special dentists' glue. For the next four weeks, Mrs Bones had to be fed with tweezers four or five

NEW ZEALAND
PASSPORT
URUWHENUA

CLASS
Aves
ORDER
Charadriiformes: waders & gulls
FAMILY
Recruvirostridae: stilts & avocets
SCIENTIFIC NAME
Himantopus novaezelandiae
COMMON NAME
Black stilt
MĀORI NAME
Kakī

Mr Bones and his new mate, C1, feeding beside the stream in the aviary.

times a day. Without her bill, she was like a person with no hands: she could not feed or preen herself, build a nest, engage in courtship with Mr Bones — everything a kaki does requires a bill.

Unfortunately, the glue only lasted two months, so it was back to the surgery again. This time, John used pins to attach the splints and the operation was a success. Mrs Bones returned to Mr Bones in the aviary and went on to lay many more eggs.

Emily Sancha, the kaki aviculturalist at Twizel, named Mrs Bones. 'Her lowest weight was 145 g. 200–220 g is normal, so she was *very* skinny — on death's doorstep. Ivan, our avicultural assistant, started to call her "Bones" and I turned it into "Mrs Bones",' Emily says.

Mrs Bones was a high-flier for the kaki recovery programme. She lived another two years before the mend failed again, but this time no one could help her. She died at the end of the breeding season in early 2002 at the age of 12. In her life she had laid a record 84 eggs, 64 of which had been successfully raised, either by her and Mr Bones or by the Kaki Captive Breeding team.

Mr Bones has since been paired with another female, C1, and the aviaries have been hung with soft sports netting so Mrs Bones' accident will never happen again.

Emily knew her really well. 'She was our best breeder by far. She's left a big gap,' she says. 'She was just so wicked! She laid so many fertile eggs. She was a really, really, strong, good-quality female. We've been incredibly lucky to have her as long as we have.'

Birds on the river

Kaki are not alone in being affected by changes to the rivers. Twenty-six other species share the kaki's world, some of them also very rare. Among them are the wrybill, oystercatcher, banded dotterel, the shore plover, the pied stilt, the black-fronted tern, the caspian tern and the black-billed gull.

Emily and Mrs Bones with her splinted beak.

Kaki problems

The rivers of the Upper Waitaki Basin are called *braided rivers*. Year by year they move from one strand to another, forming wide stony beds, lakes and pools, oxbows, kettleholes, puddles and islands. They are shallow, fast-flowing and flood often. It's a harsh world. In winter, the temperature can plunge to -30°C, and sometimes Emily finds frost on the kaki's backs in the mornings. In summer it can scorch up to 40°C. Kaki are tough. They have lived here a long, long time. It's not the weather that is killing them.

But if they are so tough, why have they almost disappeared?

The answer is that kaki without rivers and wetlands are like birds without feathers. The very places that have always been their homes for centuries, that have sheltered and fed them, are now *kaki danger zones*.

After the burning and clearing of bush, one of the biggest changes in the New Zealand landscape in the last 200 years has been the taming of rivers, swamps and wetlands, mainly for farming.

River banks have been cleared and fenced and water has been taken for irrigation. Cattle and machines squash nests, break eggs, kill chicks and frighten parent birds off their nests.

Worse, farms bring rabbits, and with rabbits come the night-hunters — rats, stoats, ferrets, cats and hedgehogs. Adult kaki are usually safe, but eggs and chicks make easy meals for hungry predators, especially in years when rabbit numbers are low.

Farmers don't like it when rivers move from place to place because it makes a mess of boundaries, fences and paddocks. So willows have been planted to hold the banks. Gorse, broom and lupins have moved in — they look pretty but they clog the river and make great hiding places for those rats, stoats, ferrets and hedgehogs.

Hydro dams have been built and rivers either drowned or dried up. Deep, straight races where kaki cannot eat or nest have been made to carry water swiftly from one place to another. Now there is too much water for kaki in some places and not enough in others — no more floods to clean the banks and no more wandering channels. Less to eat. Fewer places to nest.

Last of all, fun-seekers have come. Wide stony rivers are excellent for trout and salmon fishing, jet-boating and off-road driving. But the wake from a boat will wash a nest away and a 4WD vehicle wipes out a clutch of speckled brown eggs and drivers don't even know it.

By 1981, when DOC stepped in, there were just 23 birds left in the world. It was a wonder there were any at all.

The time of danger. Even a well-camouflaged chick and eggs can make a quick meal for a predator or can be accidentally squashed or washed away.

Kaki habitat being destroyed by cattle feeding in the wide riverbeds near Tekapo.

Candling eggs

Candling is when you shine a bright light through an egg. If it's fresh, it is quite bright and you can see the yellowness of the yolk. Above, Emily puts eggs into the incubator, and after a week she'll re-candle them. If they've turned dark, she knows a chick is growing inside, but if it still looks bright and yellow, then she knows the egg is infertile (see a picture of a candled egg on p. 91). Even then Emily is not finished. She opens the egg to find out why it is a dud, and photographs it as well.

Kaki solutions

First, DOC set up the Kaki Captive Breeding Centre to ensure kaki did not die out altogether. There are three large aviaries at Twizel, with six permanent breeding pairs. In the spring, eggs are taken from wild birds and from the captive birds and taken to the centre.

'I artificially incubate them, hatch out the chicks and hand-raise them, then we release them into the wild as juveniles at three months old or sub-adults at nine months,' Emily says. Around 80 chicks are raised but because there is only space to keep 60 once they start to grow, 20 are released early. This way, even though not all the young ones make it, there is still a big boost to wild kaki numbers. 'Short-term, it's the fastest way to avoid extinction,' Emily says.

Kaki start courting in August. In September, the male makes a few trial nests for his mate to choose from. She picks one out, helps him finish it, then, around October, she lays four brown speckled eggs.

Then along comes a DOC contractor and steals them. The kaki freak out. Sometimes they leave their first nest and build a new one. Sometimes they stay put. Then they get over it and lay more eggs . . . and along comes the DOC team again to take the eggs. More freaking out! But it's OK because this is what can happen in the wild anyway. Kaki have learned to cope with egg loss by laying more. DOC staff are just taking advantage of this.

In the aviaries, this can happen up to four times, which means one pair of birds could produce 16 chicks a year. This can be hard on the female, but she is given special food to keep her strong.

Simon Elkington carries an egg collection box across the very cold lower Cass River.

The eggs are in the incubator for 22 days.

When the last set is taken, the aviary parents are given a set of ceramic eggs, warmed and painted to look like their own. 'They incubate those eggs quite happily for three weeks,' Emily says. 'And when it's almost hatching time, I put back the real eggs that I've been keeping in the incubator. I do this because the eggs are safer in the incubator than they are in the aviary.' Kaki are too precious to take chances.

Once the chicks hatch, they are kept in breeder units with pretend kaki parents. 'The dummy bird has a heat pad on its belly and a speaker. Whenever we're moving chicks around, we play alarm calls through the dummy bird, so the chicks all freeze or go and hide,' Emily says. She and her helpers don't want the chicks to become tame or used to humans, so they keep away from them as much as possible.

In the wild, kaki chicks feed themselves from the moment they hatch. This means they will only eat food that is alive and moving — and that means Emily and the team have to hit the rivers in waders, taking nets to catch mayfly larvae and caddis fly larvae and water boatmen. 'It keeps us quite busy!' Emily says.

After 10 days, the chicks are given bought mealworms, which they love, then as they grow they move to a mix of minced ox-heart, ground up Biscats, calcium carbonate, iodised salt and vitamins.

At three months, 20 juveniles are set free. They are taken to the safe Ruataniwha wetland, the cage doors are opened and away they go. They will not all survive but with the help of DOC and the captive breeding programme they have a much better chance.

Fly away, kaki

Release day at the Ruataniwha wetland is awesome. The kaki have been able to fly in the aviaries but they've never flown free before and never so high. It's also the first time that they're all together. It's quite a reward after all the hard work.

Schools, landowners, newspaper, television, radio people and Ngai Tahu come along. Ngai Tahu regard kaki as a taonga and are part of the Kaki Recovery Group team. There is always someone to say a karakia and bless the young birds as they fly into their brave new world. *Yaayy! Go! Fly!*

Two-day old chicks feed beside their dummy kaki parent.

Ivan Andrews holds a juvenile kaki.

Kaki facts

- There are two kinds of stilt in New Zealand. One is the kaki or black stilt, *Himantopus novaezelandiae*, the other is the kaki's cousin, the poaka or pied stilt, *Himantopus himantopus leucocephalus*. Both flew here from Australia, but kaki arrived maybe a million years ago and poaka have been here about 200 years. Poaka are much more widespread because they have learned to live with predators.

- When they first arrived in New Zealand, kaki would have looked like the poaka of today. Once they were here, they changed to fit their new home. Their feathers turned black and their bills became long and strong. They grew bigger. The only danger was from above, so they learned to avoid or fight off harriers and to camouflage eggs and chicks. Instead of nesting in colonies for safety, as poaka do, pairs took to nesting by themselves. They often do this on river banks where they are mostly safe from floods — but much easier for predators to find.

- When poaka and kaki are stalked by enemies, they pretend to have broken wings to lead the killer away from their nests but this trick has not been enough to keep kaki safe.

- Kaki are one of the world's rarest birds. They are ranked as critically endangered, which means they are certain to become extinct without human help.

- From beak to tail, kaki are 380 mm long. They weigh about 220 g, about as much as a good-sized orange. They have long, long legs (the longest for their size of any bird), a long neck and a tiny body. They are very elegant.

- Kaki eat water boatmen, mayfly larvae, backswimmers, damselflies, midge larvae, small fish, grassgrubs and worms. No other wading birds have as many techniques for feeding. Observers have watched kaki plunging at prey on the river bottom, snatching at insects flying past, snapping at prey on the surface of the water, scything their beaks through muddy water for worms, probing under stones for larvae, and raking through shingle with their beaks.

- Adult kaki have striking glossy black feathers that are almost green in sunlight, bright red legs with short toes, black toenails and no hind toe, luminous orange-red eyes, a strong, straight black beak and a high-pitched voice — *kak, kak, kak!* Young kaki have black and white feathers and pink legs. They moult and darken over the first two years until they have adult colours.

- Unlike most waders, kaki generally like to stay put. They do not usually migrate to other places with the changing seasons.

- Kaki mate for life. They mostly lay four eggs, speckled to match the stones of the river, around October. Males and females nest-build together and take turns, hour on and hour off, sitting on the eggs. Chicks hatch with their eyes open and leave the nest almost straight away. They begin to feed themselves straight away too, and never get fed by their parents! Young chicks freeze if there is danger; older chicks run and hide. Chicks lose their fluff and grow feathers in about 45 days, and are ready to leave home at eight months when their parents kick them out so they can get ready to bring up the next lot.

- Kaki have inquisitive, friendly personalities, though they are also nervous and panic easily.

- In February 2003, there were 125 kaki in the wild.

Kaki in flight above the Cass River.

A predator-proof fence protects the kaki breeding area at Lake Tekapo.

A safe place for kaki

One day the Captive Breeding Centre may not be needed any more. For that to happen, kaki will need safe places to live and breed.

The 98-hectare Ruataniwha man-made wetland on a terrace above the Ohau River is the first of these. It is surrounded by a high mesh fence and electric wires. Inside, water levels are controlled to ensure plenty of food at breeding time. Ninety percent of the kaki hatched here survive to become adults, which is much, much better than outside. The wetland is also very popular with other species!

But finding an even larger area that is free of predators will not be easy, because the kaki's story is so entwined with the lives of people.

There are no suitable offshore islands, so the area will need to be on the mainland. If it's on a river, then other users — farmers, tourism operators, walkers, campers, anglers, hunters and power companies — will need to be happy about it. Like kaki, many depend on the rivers.

And it will be hard to protect. You can't fence a fast-flowing, often-flooding river. And how do you stop rats, stoats, ferrets, cats and hedgehogs if, every time you kill one, it is replaced by another from the surrounding countryside?

It's a big job, but for those who work with kaki, there is absolutely no doubt that it has to be done. These little birds are worth it, and they will find a way. It will be a great day when Mr and Mrs Bones' descendants fly and wade and breed in freedom and safety.

All blacks

New Zealand has a lot of black birds! The kaki is the only solidly black stilt in the world. Other *melanistic* birds (birds that have become black) are the oystercatcher (above), the black fantail, the black tomtit and the black robin.

Mixed marriages — no more kaki?

Although they are separate species, kaki will breed with poaka, especially when there are not enough kaki females. The chicks of these couples are slightly speckled, and are known as *hybrids*. Overall, they tend to behave more like their poaka mums. If this happened too much, kaki would become just as extinct as if they had all died from some other cause. Luckily, as the population grows and the numbers of male and female kaki equalise, that is less likely to happen.

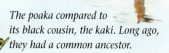

The poaka compared to its black cousin, the kaki. Long ago, they had a common ancestor.

Another river lover — whio, the blue duck

'Whiii–oo, whiii–oo.'

Most ducks like lakes or ponds, but not whio! Just like kaki, whio love rivers — the cleaner, clearer and faster the better. Whio rivers tumble and burble over rocks and boulders, through quiet pools and down small waterfalls. They are often high in the mountains and hills. Unlike the wide, open spaces of kaki rivers, it's best for whio when there is bush along the river banks, so there's somewhere for the bugs to breed that whio eat.

Whio rivers are so rough-and-tumble that whio have grown flaps on each side of their bills to protect them from knocks against stones and boulders. They also have huge rubbery feet to help them swim against that rushing, gushing water.

Like kaki, whio are endangered and protected.

This whio is vacuuming the rocks for goodies in Newton Creek, Westland, 1989.

Whio's problems

- Many of the whio river banks have been cleared of bush for farms.
- Some whio rivers have been dammed for hydro-electricity.
- Stoats, ferrets, rats and wild cats are the worst. They steal eggs and kill chicks and nesting females.
- Dogs, gulls, hawks, eels and shags also kill whio.
- Introduced trout eat the same bugs as whio which leaves less for them.
- They can be affected by the trampers, shooters and white-water rafters in the same ways as kaki.

Whew! Whii–oo!

A whio parent and three ducklings on the Manganui-a-te-ao River, near Raetihi, 1989.

The remains of a whio adult and egg beside the Manganui-a-te-ao River after a visit from a predator.

Whio facts

- Whio have bright yellow eyes and large feet. They have soft blue-grey feathers with brown-speckled chests that merge perfectly into their river backgrounds.
- Whio are named after the whistle of the male — *whii–oo, whii–oo*. It used to be a familiar sound for people walking along river banks in the bush.
- Whio have strong pair bonds. Male whio help guard and feed whio ducklings. Family groups on the river usually have one parent at each end and a string of pearly-headed ducklings in the middle.
- Whio live for about eight years. They feed on caddis fly, mayfly, stonefly larvae and freshwater snails. They nest in riverside caves, hollow logs, and beneath flax bushes. Although a number of chicks may hatch, not all will survive.
- The species is scattered over parts of both the North and South Islands. Isolated populations exist in forested river catchments in parts of the eastern and central North Island, Nelson, the West Coast and Fiordland. It is thought there are only about 400 breeding pairs left.

Read more about whio at: www.doc.govt.nz/Conservation/001~Plants-and-Animals/001~Native-Animals/Blue-Duck-(Whio).asp or at: www.cmag.org.nz/captive_blueduck.html

Bryan Williams (left) and Murray Williams are weighing and banding a whio beside the Manganui-a-te-ao River.

Homing ducks?

People are helping whio by taking them back to places where they once lived and by making those places safe.

Stoats, ferrets, rats and other predators had killed whio on Mount Taranaki in the North Island but the mountain has clear, fast-flowing rivers and as long as those whio enemies can be controlled, they should do well there.

However, no one told the ducks! The first whio did not want to stay — they flew several hundred kilometres back to their old homes, which was not what anyone expected, as whio are not considered very strong fliers.

Next time, younger birds, with a weaker homing instinct were taken from the Manganui-a-te-ao River near Raetihi. By the end of April 2003 there were 20 whio on the mountain.

Traps have been placed every 100 metres for 7 km around the release area to keep whio safe. In the three months after trapping started, two stoats, two ferrets, a weasel, two hedgehogs and 38 rats were killed.

The relocations are done with the blessing and assistance of Tamahaki Maori from the whio home area, Raetihi, and Ngati Ruanui of Taranaki.

Murray Williams is measuring a whio foot at Manganui-a-te-ao River.

4 *Sharp shooter!*
Ngakeoke, or peripatus, the worm-insect

NGAKEOKE IS A PRETTY THING. She has velvet skin, cute wee legs, a groovy way of moving, and looks a bit like a caterpillar. Who would think that she would be a sharp-shooting killer, living on other invertebrates? You wouldn't expect her to take on a spiny, spiky customer like a weta and win.

But she does. She has a secret weapon — spit!

And she has disgusting table manners.

NEW ZEALAND

PASSPORT
URUWHENUA

PHYLUM
Onychophora

GENERA
Peripatoides

COMMON NAMES
Peripatus, walking worm, velvet worm

MĀORI NAME
Ngākeoke

In the dark of night, the ngakeoke senses food walking by. It's a weta, out looking for some leaves to munch. Ngakeoke takes aim with the two pistol-like papillae in her mouth and out shoots a net of runny goo. *Glop!* In seconds the goo turns sticky, trapping the weta. It struggles but it's a goner.

When humans eat, it's a process with several steps, mechanical and chemical. First, we chew our food. This chops it up and coats it with saliva which helps break it up some more. Then we swallow it and our stomachs finish the job with enzymes that help us digest it — hungry enzymes, just like in the advertisements.

Not the ngakeoke! She makes a *stomach out of her victim*. She begins by gnawing a hole in the underside of the weta's body and pumping it full of enzyme-loaded saliva. This dissolves and partially digests the weta — from the inside. The ngakeoke has to wait a while for this to happen, but in the meantime she eats the gluey spit. Nothing is wasted. Finally, dinner is ready. She sucks out the sloppy predigested soup from the weta's body and the empty shell collapses. *Urp!* She heads away for an after-dinner *zzzzz*.

Is it a worm? Is it an insect? No! It's ngakeoke, the peripatus!

Peripatus are found in many other countries in the Southern Hemisphere, but New Zealand has more than 30 species all our own and new ones are being found all the time. They are out there in the bush, under logs and rocks, living in leaves and damp, shady places just quietly minding their own business. They can grow up to 60 mm long, although they are usually much smaller, and some are brightly patterned and coloured. However, perhaps because of their size and because they are nocturnal, not many people know about them.

Their names give us a clue as to why these are such amazing creatures. Their scientific name, *peripatus* means 'walking about', and one of their common names is *walking worm*. But ngakeoke are not worms and they are not insects — they are in-betweens.

Worms belong to a group of animals called *annelids*. This means they have many body segments, soft skin and, as we all know, no arms or legs.

Insects and related animals such as centipedes are called *arthropods*, and are further up the evolutionary ladder. Their body segments are fused to make specialised parts such as a head (six segments for that), a chest or thorax, and an abdomen. They have a tough outside skeleton and jointed legs. They are a lot more sophisticated than worms.

Ngakeoke are a bit of both. On the one hand, they have segmented bodies with soft skin — like worms! On the other, they have a head, sort-of eyes that don't see much except light and dark, and super-sensitive antennae. And their skin, if examined closely, is soft like a worm's but has a similar structure to an arthropod's.

Finally, ngakeoke have legs. Each segment in their bodies has one pair of balloony, round legs with a pair of tiny claws. New Zealand peripatus have between 13 and 16 pairs of legs, depending on the species.

It's no wonder they're sometimes called the 'missing link' — except that they're not missing. They are also called 'living fossils', because fossils that look like living ngakeoke have been found in rocks 300 million years old. Ngakeoke have been around a very, very long time indeed.

Peripatus and your teacher

Does your teacher pace up and down? If so, he or she is *peripatetic* and, just like peripatus, has connections to Aristotle, who founded the Peripatetic school of philosophy — Aristotle used to do his pacing in a place called the 'Peripatus'. But don't go calling your teachers 'worms' — or 'insects' — or you might find that they are something else altogether.

Ngakeoke benefit every time a sanctuary is created for other species, but one place in New Zealand is dedicated just to them.

In 1994 the Royal Forest and Bird Protection Society purchased a four-hectare block in Caversham Valley, Dunedin, which has a high number of ngakeoke. The reserve is a site of 'significant conservation value', and the bush has been restored in order to protect these amazing little animals with their velvet coats, balloony legs and spitting ways.

Ngakeoke facts

- Ngakeoke are between 50 mm and 60 mm long. New Zealand specimens have between 13 and 16 pairs of legs. The mouth of the ngakeoke contains mandibles for chewing as well as papillae for shooting spit.

- There are more than 30 species of ngakeoke. This includes the genus *Peripatus* as well as another, closely related genus, *Ooperipatus*. *Peripatus* give birth to live young — they carry 'eggs' inside soft membranes in their bodies. The eggs hatch at the same moment as they are laid. *Ooperipatus* lay eggs which hatch some time later.

- Ngakeoke males are much smaller than females. Individuals are thinly spread in the places where they live and don't travel far, so they do not mate often. When they do, the male places spermatophores on the skin of the female and the sperm is gradually absorbed into her body.

- Newly hatched ngakeoke are white but become coloured as they grow. Ngakeoke shed their skins every couple of weeks.

- Ngakeoke can be found across New Zealand in all sorts of places. As a genus they are not endangered, though individual species could easily be wiped out by having their habitats destroyed.

- Ngakeoke eat small animals such as termites, baby crickets, cockroaches, spiders and weta. In turn, they are themselves eaten by nocturnal birds such as kiwi, and nocturnal mammals such as hedgehogs, rats and mice. They are also eaten by larger invertebrates such as giant centipedes. And because they are such biological curiosities, they are sometimes taken by human collectors, which is bad news. They are much better off in the bush.

5 A liking for trees

A home for hoiho, the yellow-eyed penguin

Really to gain just a little understanding of birds it is necessary almost to live with them. This I have had to do with the penguins. Over a period of eleven years something like 1000 visits, involving travelling 40,000 miles by car, have been made to different colonies.

— Lance Richdale,
Wild South, p.180

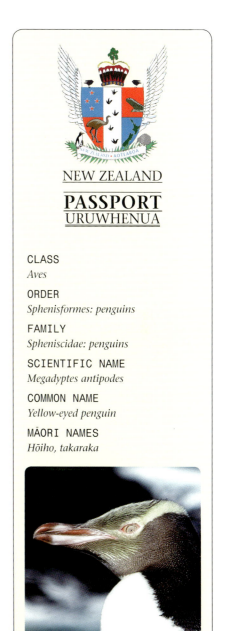

NEW ZEALAND PASSPORT URUWHENUA

CLASS
Aves

ORDER
Sphenisformes: penguins

FAMILY
Spheniscidae: penguins

SCIENTIFIC NAME
Megadyptes antipodes

COMMON NAME
Yellow-eyed penguin

MĀORI NAMES
Hōiho, takaraka

IT'S NEAR THE END OF THE DAY and everyone's going home. Schoolchildren are biking, walking, catching buses, taking trains and waiting for lifts at school gates. Everyone's tired and looking forward to home and tea.

Far out at sea, a long way from the bustle of the city, there's a sudden *plop* and a hoiho head appears. He has been diving for his favourite food, squid, sometimes as deep as 100 metres. Some days he swims up to 15 kilometres, but no matter how far he goes, he always tries to get back to land by evening.

He has to put on a spurt but as the last light touches the water, he arrows around the headland to his bay. It's south-facing and rocky, and large waves leave white claw-marks on the cliffs as they smash and drag at the coast. He swims through thick, curling kelp. Not a problem.

The hoiho leaps lightly onto a rock and waddles onto the beach. Wasting no time, he heads up the hill, his little feet bright pink in the evening light, his yellow eyes glowing. It's hard work. He has a track that goes up a steep gully and under a fence almost to the crest of a grassy hill. At times it is a tunnel through long grass, at times it crosses bare rock.

He is heading for a tall clump of flax in front of a rocky outcrop. It's not a bad spot, except that today the farmer has shifted cattle into the paddock and a huge black beast is lying about a metre from his path. It snorts and rolls its eyes at him but it doesn't stop chewing its cud.

He skirts it carefully and scuttles under the flax. The leaves curl over him and he disappears from sight.

The hoiho is the only penguin in the world to live on land all year round. Other penguins come ashore twice a year — in spring when they're hatching and raising chicks, and again when they moult. For the rest of the time, sometimes for months on end, they live at sea.

What's in a name?

Heaps, where this bird is concerned! It has three, and each one describes a different characteristic. *Hōiho*, its Maori name, means something like 'noisy shouter', referring to the calls the penguins make as they greet each other. *Yellow-eyed penguin*, its common English name, describes the mask-like crown of bright yellow that appears once the birds are about 15 months old. *Megadyptes antipodes*, its scientific name, refers to its superb ability as a swimmer and diver: *mega* = 'large' or 'great', *dyptes* = 'diver', and *antipodes* means the opposite side of the earth — usually from Britain and therefore in the southern hemisphere. So *Megadyptes antipodes* means 'great southern diver'.

A nest among tree roots at Boulder Beach on the Otago Peninsula.

When they're on land, most live in noisy colonies like little cities, with thousands of other penguins. They go for safety in numbers.

But not hoiho. Mr and Mrs Hoiho like to keep to themselves. They don't even want to *see* other hoiho. Scientists have found that if a hoiho nest is within sight of another one, then those hoiho are less likely to successfully raise chicks.

And they like to return to land most days — if they do a sleepover at sea one night, they are sure to be home the next. As night falls, all around the beaches of south-east Otago you can see them emerging from the waves and heading up the beach.

It would be easier for hoiho if their nests were close to the water among rocks or in caves, but while most other penguins have largely given up the land for the ocean, hoiho want a flipper in both camps — they still like forests. Long ago, well before humans printed their feet into the sand of New Zealand, hoiho developed a liking for tree roots, sometimes as far as a kilometre from the shore. That's a long way to walk if your legs are only a few centimetres long.

They like trees because the shade keeps them cool. Penguin feathers are like wetsuits. They trap air inside and keep the bird warm even in the iciest Antarctic or subantarctic waters. But that can be a problem on land because it doesn't take long in the sun for them to overheat.

Trees also give hoiho shelter. They snuggle in tight among the roots, safe from even the worst, wildest, windiest weather — and sometimes the weather in southern New Zealand and on the subantarctic islands where hoiho live is *very* wild and windy indeed.

Hoiho are not only the world's most ancient kind of penguin — and penguins have been around for up to 60 million years — they are also the world's rarest.

And that's partly because of the trees. For millions of years, New Zealand was covered in bush. From the slopes of the highest mountains right down to the coast, there were trees of all shapes and sizes. There were plenty of places for hoiho to live, and there was plenty of fish in the sea. That has all changed.

People like trees too. They use them to build their houses but, unlike hoiho, they are not content to just live among the roots. And they like the land beneath the trees even more.

One of the first things European settlers did when they came to New Zealand was to chop trees and burn bush to make green, grassy paddocks for sheep and cattle. Large numbers of hoiho died. Those that survived had to learn to live in gullies and scrub where sheep and cattle did not often go, places that were not as good as the trees had been.

No one intended to hurt the hoiho, and for a while they even thought hoiho and farm animals got along OK. They didn't realise that all the time there were fewer and fewer chicks and fewer and fewer penguins.

And just as with kaki, if it was bad when the trees were toppled, there was worse to come. An army of wild cats, rats, stoats, ferrets and dogs followed close behind — crafty hunting creatures with pointy noses, sharp teeth and savage claws, killers with a taste for juicy fish-fed flesh.

Grown hoiho are mostly big enough to protect themselves, but for the first weeks of their lives young hoiho are in terrible danger. Once they are adults, hoiho live for about 20 years, but when they finally grow old and die, if there are no chicks to take their places, that's it.

There are also problems for hoiho at sea. Plastic, set nets and drifting rubbish strangle and drown seabirds and other ocean creatures. If penguins get oil on their feathers from a spill, they die — they cannot swim, they cannot survive the cold and they cannot eat. No amount of preening can save them.

And then there's global warming. No one really knows what will happen if the world's climate changes, but it will almost certainly be bad for hoiho. They are near the top of a food chain. This means they feed on fish which feed on smaller fish which feed on hundreds and thousands of tiny organisms called *zooplankton*. If the world's oceans warm up, there may be less zooplankton available so all the bigger creatures, including hoiho and other kinds of penguin, will go hungry.

A hoiho parent returns to its nest on the Otago coast to find that a ferret has visited and killed and partly eaten its chick.

If that is not enough, there are other dangers. Because people now move freely around the world by air and sea, there is more chance they will accidentally import disease and harmful organisms from other parts of the world. When there are not many birds, it doesn't take much to cause a disaster such as the one that struck the hoiho on the Otago Peninsula in 2002. The population of breeding hoiho pairs fell from about 580 to 400. No one knew why but it was suspected that they had been killed by an unfamiliar bird disease.

Lance Richdale and the penguins

In 1935 a man called Lance Richdale (right) fell in love with hoiho. He spent years watching, measuring and writing about them. He drove thousands of kilometres to study them and even slept among them. He found that individual hoiho had personalities very like people. They seem to talk to each other and have a whole range of different sorts of calls and songs for different occasions.

He was fascinated by the relationships between the birds and made a list of descriptions of their 'language' — 'the Sheepish Look, the Throb, the Shake, the Gawky Look, the Open Yell, the Ecstatic Arms Act, the Bow, the Welcome, the Mutual Preen, the Kiss Preen, the Half Trumpet, and the Full Trumpet'.

Lance Richdale showed people that if they did nothing, then soon this amazing bird would be gone.

As a result, a number of things have happened:

- Parts of the coastline have been fenced, and predators have been trapped and removed. There are now safe places for hoiho.
- Reserves have been created, like the Forest and Bird Society hoiho sanctuary at Te Rere in the Catlins (south-east Otago) where flax and shrubs have been planted to re-establish nesting areas. Unfortunately another wildlife enemy, *fire*, swept through Te Rere in 1995, killing almost half the penguins. It was a tragedy, and the hoiho there are only slowly recovering.
- Schools and children raise money to help hoiho by saving Mainland Cheese stickers and holding mufti days. They also plant trees and flax to make new hoiho homes. In 1987 the Yellow-eyed Penguin Trust was formed to help look after the yellow-eyed penguin and its living places.
- Landowners are fencing cattle away from hoiho areas and working with DOC to help control hoiho enemies.
- Set nets are banned in places where they are likely to catch and kill penguins and dolphins.
- Further south, DOC works hard to keep predators off the subantarctic islands where the biggest populations of hoiho live. They study hoiho and work with other people and community groups to help hoiho.
- It is illegal to harm or kill hoiho.

Hoiho facts

- Hoiho are endemic to New Zealand. That means they breed nowhere else in the world. They live on the south-east coast of the South Island, on Stewart Island, and on the subantarctic Auckland Islands and Campbell Island.

- Hoiho are the only members of the genus *Megadyptes*. They are New Zealand's tallest penguin — up to 60 cm tall. The male is usually larger than the female. They weigh between 5.4 and 5.7 kg.

- They eat squid and sprats and small fish such as red cod and opal fish.

- They have a white tummy and a blue back, tail and flippers. They can't fly, of course, but are brilliant swimmers. Apart from the yellow crown and eyeband which gives them their English name, they also have bright pink feet! And bright yellow eyes — *definitely!*

This little fellow was photographed at Waterfall Bay on the Otago Peninsula. You can see how thick and soft his downy coat is.

Does a penguin think? What does it think? This juvenile hoiho on Enderby Island, in the Auckland Islands, looks as if it is thinking about the day when it will swim away to sea.

If they make it through the dangerous first year, hoiho chicks become handsome adults like the penguin above, trekking up the cliffs of the Otago Peninsula to get to its nest.

A year in the life of a hoiho

Hoiho mate in mid-August and September and make their nests in a shady, sheltered spot. Nests are made from dry grass and leaves, and are protected on one side by a tree, rocks, logs or flax.

Both parents share the tasks of incubating the two greenish-white eggs and then, after 43 days, of guarding and feeding the chicks. There's a lot of noise when one parent returns from a day at sea and greets the other parent before feeding the chicks. This stage lasts for six weeks, then the danger time really starts.

The chicks grow so fast and are so hungry that both parents must leave them to go fishing. But if all goes well and they are not killed by predators, the chicks will have replaced their soft down covering with waterproof feathers by early March. They leave home and travel up to 500 km north to winter feeding grounds. Many will never return — fewer than 15 percent of chicks reach breeding age.

However, once they do, they remain in the same area and may live up to 20 years.

Meanwhile the parents have a couple of weeks to feed themselves up after the hard work of chick-rearing, then they must come ashore again, this time to moult. They lose all their feathers and grow a brand-new set. This process takes three to four weeks, and during this time they cannot go to sea to feed. But once they have their new feathers, in May, they can look forward to a couple of months' feeding and getting ready for the next breeding season.

Oh, the indignity! A modern bird's life includes wearing identifying leg bands and being caught and weighed now and then by someone like Peter Moore, from DOC.

6 **The rock group**
The very secret world of Hamilton's frog

EEEET! THE TINY BROWN FROG protests as Derek Brown picks it up. Derek is belly-down on a boardwalk. There is no moon and the island is veiled by mist and cloud. He is wearing a headlamp and has a small torch jammed between his teeth. He is in the shadow of a hollow, but down the hill not far away a giant solar-powered beam circles a lighthouse. The rest of the island is still and dark.

Derek shines his light on the frog. It is tiny in the palm of his hand. 'My goodness!' he says in amazement as he reads its marked toes. 'Frog 2! I haven't seen you in such a long time! We thought you were dead!'

He wriggles to get at his camera and lines her up. They both blink at the flash. 'And look!' he says. 'You've grown so much! You look so well!' He carefully measures her and scribbles in the notebook hanging from his neck. He is finished, but he pauses for a minute. They look at each other.

Then gently, he lets her go.

NEW ZEALAND
PASSPORT
URUWHENUA

CLASS
Amphibia

SCIENTIFIC NAME
Leiopelma hamiltoni

COMMON NAME
Hamilton's frog

MĀORI NAMES FOR NEW ZEALAND FROGS
Pepeketua, pekepeke, peketua, tūpeke, ngai kura

New Zealand has over 700 islands and countless lakes, rivers, swamps and streams but Hamilton's frogs are found only in one very small place — a rock jumble in a hollow almost at the top of the highest peak of Takapourewa (Stephens Island). It is harsh and barren, with no running or standing water, and winds scream and howl overhead. The only moisture is rain and mist which soon dries away. Just by chance, however, the pile of chunky, shoebox-sized boulders where the frogs live is so deep that right at the bottom, even in the worst droughts, it is cool and damp. You would *never* expect to find frogs in this place.

But you can because Takapourewa is a fortress. It is ringed by cliffs that rise hundreds of metres from foaming, crashing seas. For hundreds of millions of years it was the kingdom of birds and small animals. It was like a mini-New Zealand. Wind-shaped trees grew on the island's back, seabirds nested on its cliffs and a group of unique birds and animals evolved, each with its own special place in this world.

That changed in 1892. Takapourewa is at the top of the South Island, in Cook Strait. It was a danger to passing ships.

'We must have a warning!' people declared. So they chopped down the bush and built a lighthouse and houses and made grassy paddocks. Three keepers and their families moved in, bringing

The cats of Takapourewa

How did one cat turn into so many? No one is sure, but it is said that another lighthouse keeper's family also brought a cat with them. It was in a sack and when the keeper's child opened the sack, the frightened cat escaped and became wild. Unfortunately, it was a pregnant female. Hundreds of cats were shot before they were finally hunted out.

Until then, they ate anything and everything, including the tuatara when they ran out of birds. Once the cats were gone, the tuatara recovered quite quickly but it was too late for some species.

The Stephens Island wren

New Zealand's four wrens were among the most primitive flying birds known. The rock wren and rifleman are still with us, but the bush wren and Stephens Island wren, *Traversia lyalli*, are gone. The Stephens Island wren had short, rounded wings and soft plumage. It was totally flightless. One of the lighthouse keepers, David Lyall, reported that they lived among the rocks and ran about like mice.

The boulder bank on Stephens Island in the 1950s. Since that time it has become a lot more overgrown and harder to see.

grazing animals for a small farm. The story goes that one of the keepers, David Lyall, also had a cat, but actually there was more than one and soon they were running wild. They had a carnival. It was such fun, chasing and killing things that fluttered and hopped.

Almost immediately, people realised what was happening and tried to get rid of the cats, but it was too late — they were out of the bag! Thirty-five years passed before they were eradicated. Fourteen species of land birds had disappeared from the island, including the Stephens Island wren, the South Island kokako and the South Island thrush. A carnivorous land snail and a large beetle were also gone, and other species were dangerously low in numbers. These included the Cook Strait giant weta, the Stephens Island ngaio weevil, the tuatara — and the very small, very secretive Hamilton's frog.

Hamilton's frogs had been first noticed in 1915. Over the years to 1942 there were occasional glimpses and then — nothing. Had they also been wiped out by the cats? In 1950 the small group at the boulder bank was discovered. They had been there all along, protected by their stony home.

Hamilton's frogs are the rarest frogs in the world. Derek Brown, the herpetologist who has been keeping an eye on them since 1987,

thinks there may be about 200 adults. The frogs are so secretive, it is really hard to tell. (A *herpetologist*, by the way, is someone who studies reptiles and amphibians.)

Four times a year, Derek travels to Takapourewa by fast boat for two hours from Havelock in the Marlborough Sounds. Sometimes he has an assistant but mostly he is alone. He spends eight to 10 days checking the frogs — making sure the adults are OK and counting the young ones. It is only by monitoring and recording a population that scientists are able to determine how best to look after it.

Landing on the island is tricky. Derek has to leap from the prow of the pitching boat onto a rocky shelf. Sometimes the sea is so rough this is not possible and the boat has to wait offshore for calm. If it's *really* bad it turns back, but this doesn't happen often. From the shelf he climbs a steep path to the lighthouse cottages.

Once on shore, Derek disinfects his shoes in case they are carrying any disease or fungus that might harm Takapourewa's creatures, and changes into clothes and boots that are never taken off the island.

The frogs are nocturnal, so he waits for dark. As he walks uphill to their rockpile, there are seabirds all around. He has to make sure he does not step on tuatara, *Sphenodon guntheri* which are everywhere. There are high, steep cliffs alongside. It sounds dangerous.

'No-o,' says Derek. 'There's a reasonably good track and the cliffs have scrubby vegetation that would in most places stop you falling more than a few feet. It's generally quite safe, though some volunteers are amazed in the daytime to see where they have walked at night! The biggest problem is strong gusty winds that have knocked me off my feet many times. Fortunately they always blow onshore, pushing me away from the edge . . .'

The frog zone is out of bounds to anyone except Derek and his helpers. Tuatara are especially unwelcome because they eat anything smaller than themselves. Frogs? *Yum*. A 1.2-metre fence with 15-mm mesh and a smooth cap keeps them out. Derek climbs into the enclosure and onto the boardwalk which protects the boulders while the frogs are being studied.

Then the search begins.

Hamilton's frogs only come to the surface of the rockpile when it is damp or humid. There is always a chance that Derek will not see them.

The slender, golden-brown frogs are very, very small, up to 49 mm long — about as long as two side-by-side 10-cent pieces. Juveniles may be only 12 mm long, the size of a little fingernail. They do not have earholes and are silent. No *knee-deep-knee-deep* or *readit-readit* jokes for these chaps! They have excellent camouflage, with black

How do you tell one frog from another?

Amphibians and reptiles are identified by marking the outer tips of the toes in different combinations. Leiopelma have four toes on their front feet and five on the back. Photographs are also taken, as the pattern on the upper edge of the mouth is believed to be as unique as a fingerprint.

Frog 2, the frog Derek was so pleased to see, was the second frog ever marked. She has a toe code 4-4-5-4, which means: the fourth (outer) toe on each of the front feet, the outer toe on the left rear, and the fourth from inside on the right rear. Toe codes are read from the inside to the outside on each foot, always in the same order — left front, right front, left rear, right rear. Frog 2 was marked as a 27-mm sub-adult in 1990 and not found again until 2001, when she was a large and healthy 46 mm.

Takapourewa (Stephens Island), the only place in the world where Hamilton's frog is found. You can see the lighthouse and the steep cliffs.

and dark-brown markings, and they freeze when danger is about. You have to know what you are looking for.

'They're just so difficult to find,' Derek says. 'We marked one frog in 1990 and didn't see it again for *12 years*. And then it popped up within a foot of where we had originally caught it!'

As part of his survey, Derek also checks out another site. A few years ago, an artificial rock jumble was built in a nearby patch of bush. Twelve frogs were transferred in order to create a second population. 'Some of them stayed and bred,' Derek says, 'but some disappeared almost immediately. Two actually ended up back at the original habitat 70 metres away! So they have a homing instinct which we were totally unaware of.'

At least one juvenile has since become an adult there. And there could be more, but he hasn't seen them. *'They are just so difficult to find!'*

Right now, in 2003, the Hamilton's frog population of Takapourewa seems stable. They live for an average of 12 to 15 years and are slow-breeding, but in the last few years it has seemed that the population is increasing.

In time, if scientists are confident it can be done safely, the frogs will be reared in captivity and additional groups will be established on other islands. But shifting even one frog when there are so few is a big risk and a great deal of care must be taken.

On the other hand, while there is only one group of the frogs, there is continuing risk anyway. Frog populations around the world, including another precious New Zealand amphibian, the Archey's frog, have been attacked by a fungus which damages the animal's sensitive skin and either suffocates or poisons it. No one knows what has caused its deadly spread. Is it air pollution? Is it a change in the atmosphere? Is it global warming? Is it something that has always been there and has suddenly worsened? Is it the scientists themselves? Is it a mix of these factors?

And what can be done about it? How do you help something so small and so fragile? As Kermit would say — *it's not easy, being green* — or maybe he should say — *brown!*

This picture of a Hamilton's frog is about the same size as the real thing.

Frog facts

- Frogs are amphibians. In evolutionary terms, that means they have never quite achieved the ability to live completely out of the water. They must keep their skins damp, and their young go through a gilled fish-like stage (tadpole) before they turn into four-legged, lung-breathing, land-dwelling adults.

- Hamilton's frog is one of four New Zealand native frogs. The first, Hochstetter's frog or *Leiopelma hochstetteri*, is semi-aquatic and lives near or in water. The other three, Hamilton's frog or *Leiopelma hamiltoni*, Archey's frog or *Leiopelma archeyi*, and the Te Hoiere (Maud Island) frog or *Leiopelma pakeka*, are terrestrial — they live in damp places but not necessarily in or near standing or running water. They don't even swim like other frogs — they use an ungainly dog-paddle rather than breast-stroke.

  Leiopelma hamiltoni and *Leiopelma pakeka* are very similar, and were not described as separate species until 1998. Suddenly Hamilton's frogs were seen to be very rare indeed.

- Leiopelma are the most primitive frogs in the world. Just like tuatara, they have been in this country for millions of years and, just like tuatara, they survived long after their kind died out elsewhere.

  They have ribs which are not fused to their spines, and tail-wagging muscles — but no tails to wag. They have no vocal sacs — although they give a chirp sometimes when they are handled. They also have no external ear openings — but they do have inner ear bones and may hear some sound. They have no webs between their toes.

- Leiopelma get around the lack of water by going through their tadpole stage inside a jelly-like egg capsule! Ten to 12 eggs are laid and the tadpole stage takes place inside the egg. When they hatch, very tiny frogs, complete with tail and yolk sac, come out. The tail and yolk sac disappear in a few weeks.

  The male frogs are active parents. They sit over the eggs once they are laid and look after the froglets, which sometimes ride on their backs. The froglets take about four years to become adults.

- Leiopelma are nocturnal and carnivorous. They feed on small insects and other invertebrates. Most frogs' tongues are anchored at the front, meaning that they can catch their prey with a *quick flick*, but not leiopelma — their tongues are anchored at the back and they lunge at prey with open mouths.

- All leiopelma are completely protected by law.

Did you hear the one about . . .

. . . this frog that goes into a bank and approaches the teller. He can see from her nameplate that her name is 'Patricia Whack'. So he says, 'Ms Whack, I'd like to get a loan to buy a boat and go on a long holiday.' Patti looks at the frog in amazement.

'How much do you need?' she asks.

'$30,000,' says the frog.

'You had better give me your details,' she says.

'Yeah, sure,' says the frog. 'I'm Kermit Jagger. My dad is Mick. It's OK. I know the bank manager.'

'Well, yes,' says Patti. 'But $30,000 is a lot of money. Do you have anything for security?'

'Sure,' says Kermit. 'I have this.' And he produces a tiny porcelain elephant, about 12 mm tall, bright pink and perfectly formed.

Patti takes the little elephant and goes to the manager.

'Excuse me,' she says. 'There's a frog called Kermit Jagger out there who claims to know you, and wants to borrow $30,000. And he wants to use this as security.'

She holds up the pink elephant and says, 'I mean, what the heck is this?'

The bank manager looks back at her and says, 'It's a knick knack, Patti Whack, give the frog a loan. His old man's a Rolling Stone!'

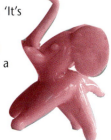

7 Grey ghosts & shadows

The haunting song of the South Island kokako

I just wanted the birds saved from extinction but you can't manage birds that refuse to be found.

— Rhys Buckingham,
Forest & Bird, August 1989

South-west Stewart Island, 1984

THOKKER-THOKKER-THOK. It is late afternoon and the bush is dripping from all-day, non-stop rain. The kokako is feeding in a tall rimu tree and he hears the helicopter long before it appears behind the hills. He is a beautiful bird, pearly blue-grey with an inky-black Beagle Boy mask and contrasting orange wattles below his beak. He watches the helicopter land on the beach. Three men emerge and unload boxes and bags, then one of them gets back in. *Thokker-thokker-thok.* The helicopter flies away.

The two remaining men climb the hill to the flat space below the bird's tree.

'This is it,' says one of them. 'Kokako central! Makes a good base. Sheltered from the wind.'

'Yes,' says the other one. 'Nice view as well.'

The bird moves into the leaves. He has seen people before and is nervous but curious. He watches the men erect a tent and make camp before hopping through the branches and away for the night.

He is on the move before sunrise next morning, hungry for a feed of berries, leaves and the occasional insect. He sees the men under the tree, yawning and stretching, moving by torchlight. He hears the murmur of their voices. He keeps his distance. They shoulder packs and tramp off around the bay and he silently continues feeding.

It rains again all day, and by the time the men come back in the evening a cold wind is flicking at the bay. They move around, cooking, eating, cleaning up for the night, then go into the tent. He hears the *zzip* of the mosquito screen and watches their shapes moving against the light. They are talking quietly.

'Listen to this,' says one. 'Got these calls here last year, but could we ever see it? No way! Never saw a sign. We called it *Titus the Ghost Bird.* It was always there, very close and often calling very loudly but we just could not see it. Listen.'

The bird is startled. It is his own call, although he does not know

NEW ZEALAND
PASSPORT
URUWHENUA

CLASS
Aves

ORDER
Passeriformes: perching birds

FAMILY
Callaeidae: New Zealand wattlebirds

SCIENTIFIC NAMES
North Island kokako:
  Callaeas cinerea wilsoni
South Island kokako:
  Callaeas cinerea cinerea

COMMON NAMES
Blue-wattled crow, blue gill, orange-wattled crow, organ-bird

MĀORI NAME
Kōkako

it, loud and clear. He bounces from branch to branch, excited but wary, until he is above the tent.

The call comes again, a two-note sliding chime, like the peal of a bell. Immediately, he answers, just one note. *Hello?*

For a second there is a stunned silence and then it is like an explosion in the tent below. There is a clatter and the *zzzitt!* of the mosquito screen as the two men burst into the evening. They are looking up at the tree, the rain running down their faces, their jackets rapidly becoming soaked. The bird keeps stone-still, his steel-grey feathers and black mask a perfect camouflage.

'It's up there! Just there!' one of the men says in a loud whisper.

'Yeah, but can you see it?'

'No.'

For a long time they peer upwards and the bird keeps very still, looking back. No one makes a sound.

'Play it again!' the first man whispers. The other presses the button on his tape recorder and the bird hears the call, *his call*. Without pause he replies — one loud, clear note.

'Look!' says the first man, pointing. 'I think I see it! Just there!'

The bird takes fright and with a brief *thwhirr*, is gone.

The man rubs his eyes. 'Goddam it,' he says. 'I *think* I saw it. Did you?'

The other man shakes his head and laughs. 'Nope,' he says. 'But that would have been him, all right. *Titus the never-seen.*'

The story of the South Island kokako is a mystery to rival that of the search for the kakapo or the finding of the takahe. It is the tale of a bird so shy, so secretive that it has *never ever* been photographed alive. It is a grey spectre hopping through the lives of the people who search for it, a mist that your hand passes through as you reach towards it or a rainbow that is always somewhere ahead.

New Zealand has two subspecies of kokako, one on each side of Cook Strait. Long-time kokako seekers Rhys Buckingham and John Kendrick believe the South Island kokako, *Callaeas cinerea cinerea* are so different from the North Island kokako, *Callaeas cinerea wilsoni*, that they are a separate species — or would be, if someone could find a South Island kokako to make a comparison. No one can be sure because they just don't want to be, *will not be* found.

Rhys first searched for the South Island kokako in 1980 soon after

'I remember our first experiences of the kokako — just hearing it. I heard it for quite a long time before I actually saw one. It had the most exquisite sound. There'd be a great impenetrable greenness all round, of tawa leaves, and you couldn't work out where the sound was coming from — but the air would fill with the most beautiful, haunting song with a somewhat melancholy note at the end. Later I actually saw the birds, and they were so different from any other birds that I'd ever seen in the New Zealand forest — with their strange, almost falling motion when they were flying, and the extraordinary, almost monkey-like agility with which they ran around in the forest on those long legs. I knew they were of rare and ancient origin and I felt I was in the presence of something . . . quite otherworldly. One had the feeling of walking back into something enormously peaceful and still and ancient.'

— Guy Salmon
Wild South, p. 210

he left university. He spent three months by himself in the bush of Stewart Island and heard unforgettable bell calls that were unlike those of any bird he knew. They were teasing, tantalising, beautiful. They had to be kokako, but he had no proof.

Two years later, in the Catlins, he glimpsed one. He was looking into the light and saw the outline of a bird as it ran up a log, hopped off and — *whit!* — disappeared. *What was that?* He could hardly believe it, but 20 minutes later he heard three chimes and knew for sure that it had been a South Island kokako.

Rhys is not the kind of person to let something go. He is absolutely certain the birds are still out there. He has spent a lot of time taping and tracking their North Island cousins so he knows his kokako calls — the clucks and twangs, cat meows and flute songs.

'You get up early and the North Island kokako are singing and so you go over to where they are. No problem,' he says. But South Island kokako are much harder. 'They rarely produce more than three notes — quite often, it's just one and then you have to wait half an hour to hear another couple. They are just so incredibly reticent and hard to find.'

Rhys, John and others have made countless find-the-kokako expeditions in all parts of the South Island. Once, someone found a kokako feather, but then it was lost when sent overseas for testing. Another time a bushman taped a song so definitely kokako that Rhys nearly fell off his chair when he heard it — but that too was lost, in a house fire. He and John have listened to fishers, hunters and trampers who tell of fleeting grey shapes and songs without singers. Sometimes sightings turn out to be birds like tui, but often Rhys knows this is the real thing and then, if he can, he is off to check it out.

Sometimes in the last few years, he has begun to doubt, to wonder if his quarry is slipping away. He has been searching for over 20 years, and John has been searching far longer. Much time and money has been spent and they are no closer than when they started. It is very likely now that the few kokako heard are lone males, living out their lives long after females and chances of breeding are gone. Kokako live for 20 or more years. Perhaps the quest should be abandoned? *But then the phone rings.*

'Is that Rhys?' a caller says. 'I was down on the West Coast and I heard this most amazing song . . .'

Wot are wattles?

Wattles are brightly coloured lobes of flesh just below the beak. They are used for showing off! 'Wattlebirds mate for life,' John Kendrick says. 'When a pair have been feeding apart and come back together, they recognise each other by a small ceremony where they bow and give this lovely little series of organ-like notes and their wattles splay out in display position.' A bit like a curtsey.

Video crims

Who killed the kokako chicks? In 1995 video cameras were placed on 19 nests for 24 hours to find out. In the video record from one nest there were two chicks and a female parent at the start.

First, there were seven rat visits, one after the other. They may have been seven different rats, or they may have been the same one, seven times. Each time the invader was repelled by the nesting female. Then there was a possum visit, but he was just having a nosey and didn't hurt the chicks. Two more rat visits followed which were again fought off.

Next, a harrier hawk came and the female had to escape for her life. The harrier killed and ate one chick and the other jumped from the nest and died on the ground. Two more rat visits followed, with the rats looking for leftovers. The harrier came back the next day, just in case there was anything more. By then, the female and male kokako had given up. They abandoned the nest and did not lay any more eggs that season.

A four-day-old North Island kokako chick at Mapara Wildlife Reserve. This little bird was luckier than the ones in the story!

The most obvious difference between the South Island kokako and its northern cousin is that it has orange wattles instead of blue. However, Rhys Buckingham and John Kendrick believe their behaviour is also quite different, and that is why the South Island kokako are so hard to find and help. Both were widespread throughout New Zealand in pre-human times and both have become very rare. But unless something dramatic happens, South Island kokako are doomed to follow their cousins, the huia, into extinction, while North Island kokako have a good chance of being long-term survivors.

There are 1200 North Island kokako in the wild. They live in a number of different locations. Three things threaten their survival.

The first, destruction of their forest homes by logging or clearance, is slowing and has nearly stopped. People have begun to value forests and trees as never before since humans arrived in New Zealand.

The second is competition, especially from possums. Kokako and possums eat almost the same things, so it is a seesaw — possum numbers up, kokako numbers down. And vice versa. Other bush-munchers, such as goats, are almost as bad.

The third problem is the constant one of predation. Kokako on the hop look after themselves quite well but ship rats, possums, stoats and harriers are all fierce and hungry killers — eggs, chicks and nesting females are easy game.

In 1991 DOC published the *Kokako Recovery Plan*. With the help of State Insurance Ltd and Norwich Union Group, they placed back-up kokako on offshore islands such as Little Barrier, Tiritiri Matangi and Kapiti. They also put lots of effort into trapping and killing the rats, stoats and possums in the places where the kokako still lived.

It made a huge difference. In kokako forests such as Te Urewera National Park in the Bay of Plenty, the Hunua Ranges near Auckland, Mount Bruce National Wildlife Centre in the Wairarapa and Mapara Forest in the King Country, the tide turned almost immediately.

Of course, the possums, rats and stoats don't go away. They still need to be controlled. But it's good to know that, with a little help, the songs of *these* birds will not yet fade into the trees and mist and hills of yesterday.

Kokako at Boundary Stream

Sarah King runs the kokako captive breeding programme at Boundary Stream Reserve, north of Napier. Boundary Stream falls through bush from a 1000-metre mountain range inland to a huge waterfall at 300 metres. There are five pairs of kokako which were captured in the bush of Te Urewera and taken to Boundary Stream. They are kept in large, well-separated aviaries at the centre.

'Catching them was a huge job,' Sarah says. 'It took 11 days to get the first three pair and then another seven to catch the other two.' In the picture at right, Sarah releases one of the transferred kokako into the aviary at Boundary Stream Reserve. It had just been flown from Te Urewera by helicopter.

When Sarah started she was determined not to get too fond of the kokako or to humanise them by giving them names. But she is finding it hard because, she says, 'The birds are all so different. They are real characters and you can't help yourself!'

The kokako have been at Boundary Stream Reserve for two years now and are still getting used to their new environment. They have not yet bred, but next spring should see the first kokako to hatch in Hawke's Bay for over 100 years — a major cause for celebration.

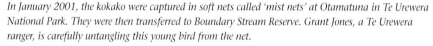

In January 2001, the kokako were captured in soft nets called 'mist nets' at Otamatuna in Te Urewera National Park. They were then transferred to Boundary Stream Reserve. Grant Jones, a Te Urewera ranger, is carefully untangling this young bird from the net.

Megan Ward is looking at a juvenile kokako being held by Jeff Hudson of DOC Opotiki. It has just had a transmitter attached to its back.

Kokako facts

- Kokako are the largest surviving New Zealand songbirds. They live in the same territories all year, and sing at dawn from the highest point to let their next-tree neighbour kokako know to keep their distance, then they glide to lower levels to feed. Because they don't travel to find food, they have learned to eat what is available and so will take up to 60 or 70 different foods from all parts of the bush. Berries are choice but kokako also eat leaves, insects, flowers and buds, depending on the season and what is around.

- Kokako are the monkeys of the New Zealand bush! They are dark blue-grey, around 380 mm long and weigh about 230 g. Males and females are similar to look at, but males are a little larger. They are weak fliers with short, rounded wings. Instead, they have powerful legs and hop and bounce through the branches just like their mammal equivalents. They also usually eat standing on one leg, holding food to their bills with the other.

- It was once thought that kokako mated for life but it now seems that they swap around every few years. They first breed at two years old. Their nests are large twig constructions with smaller moss-lined cups in the top. They lay three cream, brown-speckled eggs which the female incubates. She also broods the chicks, which is why there are fewer females in some population groups — they are more vulnerable on the nest. They live for about 20 years.

- New Zealand wattlebirds are not related to Australian wattlebirds, which are honey-eaters. They are also not crows, although they were called that by early settlers.

- Like New Zealand's other unique birds, the wrens and the native thrush, kokako ancestors were in this country as long ago as 65 million years.

North Island kokako adults feeding their chicks with orange berries. You can see the pink wattles of the chicks.

Huia and tieke

There were once three species of New Zealand wattlebird — the huia, the kokako and the tieke, or saddleback.

Huia were handsome magpie-sized blue-black birds. They were weak fliers like kokako and lived in the deep forest. They had orange wattles and a white bar across the end of their tails that made the feathers prized by the Maori and later, by Europeans. It's said that in 1902 the Duke of York wore a huia tail feather in his hatband. This started a craze, the feathers became very valuable, and good money could be made by shooting just one bird. They were also shot in large numbers for collectors.

Huia were unusual because they were the only bird species in the world where males and females had very different bills — the male's was about 60 mm long, straight, strong and pointed, and the female's was about 104 mm and curved. He ate grubs in the outside of rotten logs while she scoffed grubs in the middle just like Jack Sprat and his missus.

Huia were legally protected from 1892 but that didn't protect them. The last living huia were seen in 1907.

Tieke are black with orange wattles and chestnut-orange saddles on their shoulders and backs. They eat invertebrates, fruit and nectar.

Like the kokako and huia, tieke were once found throughout New Zealand but disappeared from the mainland islands over 100 years ago. By 1950 they were found only on Hen Island in the north and on three islands off Stewart Island in the south. Things did not look good for them, but some were moved to safe islands and they have since done so well that on 16 June 2002, 39 North Island tieke were flown from Tiritiri Matangi to the Karori Wildlife Sanctuary in Wellington — another cause for celebration.

A tieke, or saddleback, showing the bright feathers across its shoulders.

Climbing trees

One of a DOC worker's jobs is putting bands on birds' legs. The colours and order of the bands are how the birds are identified, and are how scientists learn where birds go, who they mate with and how long they live. But in order to band a kokako you have to catch it and that's not easy!

Which is why bands are put on the legs of fledglings before they leave the nest. People like Sarah King get to be excellent rope and ladder and tree climbers. 'One time,' Sarah says, 'we could see this kokako nest right at the top of a thin tawa tree. We could only get a rope to half way so I had to free-climb all the rest using a safety harness. So up I went and I got to the top and the tree was swaying to one side and then the other. I finally got there — and there was nothing in the nest — they'd gone! All that effort and sweat and fear . . . *oh!*'

8 Blue blood on the mountain
Powelliphanta, the giant snail of Taranaki

TONIGHT, JIM CLARKSON, the DOC ranger at Egmont National Park, will sleep well. He's been up since daybreak, walked mountain tracks for more than three hours, scrambled in and out of, over and under thick, tangly scrub and despite head-to-toe protective clothing, is covered in scratches and cuts. When he takes a shower, it really stings.

But he loves it! His work is incredibly exciting. And because it's so hard, it's all the more rewarding. Jim has been hunting powelliphanta, or giant snails.

Jim gets up early. He collects his colleague Dean Caskey from his home, and in half an hour they drive through the stone gates at the entrance to the park. The road is sealed but narrow, and climbs steadily between walls of tall, mossy trees. By the time they reach the North Egmont Visitor Centre at 958 metres, the trees are smaller and stunted by wind and cold.

This is where most vehicles stop but Jim and Dean drive another 220 metres higher, up a steep, narrow track. They park a short distance below Tahurangi Hut. Now they are in the subalpine zone and the trees have become shrub and tussock. They tramp around the mountain, crossing a steep bluff, descending into valleys and climbing again to sharp ridges.

An hour and a half later they arrive in the powelliphanta area. It is nearly ten o'clock and they know they don't have long. They plot a line through the scrub and start searching.

The powelliphanta are nocturnal, and hide during the day in leaf litter under the dense cover of leatherwood, red tussock, grasses, ferns and alpine herbs. It's impossibly impassable! 'You use your hands more than your eyes,' Jim says. Mostly he and Dean search by feel, which is why they wear long-sleeved overalls taped at the wrists and polypropylene gloves. Even so, they get scratched and scraped.

The powelliphanta are well spread out. Hours pass and they have found nothing. They stop for a bite.

'Do you think we'll crack 70 this year?' Jim asks.

Dean laughs. They have a long-standing ambition to find the largest Taranaki powelliphanta on record. Giant land snails in other parts of New Zealand can reach 100 mm in diameter but the biggest Taranaki specimen remains a stubborn half-millimetre short of Jim and Dean's target, at 69.5 mm.

'Fat chance,' says Dean. 'Find a snail first!'

They start looking again.

Suddenly Dean gives a shout. His fingers have closed around a smooth spiral shell. He holds it up and Jim reaches for his measuring

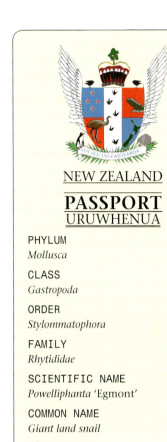

NEW ZEALAND

PASSPORT
URUWHENUA

PHYLUM
Mollusca

CLASS
Gastropoda

ORDER
Stylommatophora

FAMILY
Rhytididae

SCIENTIFIC NAME
Powelliphanta 'Egmont'

COMMON NAME
Giant land snail

MĀORI NAME
Pūpū nui

Snails on a volcano

There have been four major volcanic eruptions in the Taranaki province in the last 1.75 million years, each hundreds of thousands of years apart.

The last of these is the mountain that is also called 'Taranaki'. It first erupted around 120,000 years ago. It has never completely settled down and at times has spewed gas, mud and ash over the countryside, causing massive fires and destruction. Its most recent eruption was in 1755. At 2518 metres, Mount Taranaki is the second-highest peak in the North Island.

Mount Taranaki is like a biological island, surrounded by a sea of farmland. It has its own mix of plants, birds, insects — and, of course, snails. In 2000, Egmont National Park, which surrounds the mountain, turned 100.

The Taranaki snails are named *Powelliphanta* 'Egmont'. They were found in 1962 and will one day be registered as a separate species. 'Egmont' is a temporary name. They are the largest powelliphanta in the North Island.

Powelliphanta shells are flat and carried sideways like the one in the picture on p. 58.

callipers. This powelliphanta won't break the record. It's 58 mm.

They measure it quickly. It must not dry out. It's a dark golden-brown and glossy with moisture, but if they leave it out of its damp, leafy home for too long it will change to a lighter colour.

'The snail will actually come out of its shell and try and make an escape to somewhere wetter. It's a bit like torture for them!' Jim says.

They record its statistics and carefully return it to its place on the ground. Then, taking care not to walk on it, they keep searching.

Late in the afternoon, Jim finds three powelliphanta eggs. They are quite large, 10 to 13 mm, hard, ivory-white and oval like small birds' eggs. He measures them too and puts them back.

By now the sun has left the ridge and the mountain is becoming cold. It's time to go home. Ahead, they have a long walk back to their vehicle, much of it uphill. They shoulder their packs and set off. They will be back tomorrow.

Jim has a big job. Egmont National Park is a forest reserve of 33,527 hectares. But for five days each year, Jim zeroes in on just 35 of those hectares.

It's in May, when the south winds are becoming icy and the mountain peak is often white with snow, that Jim and Dean check the powelliphanta on the mountain. They've done this since 1996, and look forward to it. It's interesting to see how the snails are doing. Jim and Dean want to be sure they haven't been gobbled by rats, nibbled by stoats, buried in rock falls or swept away by heavy rains.

The powelliphanta are high up the mountain, in the mixed tussock-shrub meadows, about 1200 metres above sea level. It is thought that there may be as few as 700.

No one really knows how they came to be here. They may be survivors of a once-larger population that lived on tussockland around the mountain long ago, before the forests grew. Or the rest of Taranaki's powelliphanta may have been wiped out by huge volcanic eruptions in 1500 and 1755. It is thought that, just by chance, dust and ash from the volcano did not fall in this area.

Or it could also be that powelliphanta elsewhere in the region have disappeared because of predators and land clearance, leaving this population alone on its mountain island. Luckily, 1200 metres is mostly too high for rats, stoats and possums.

Measuring a powelliphanta.

Powelliphanta facts

- New Zealand has around 1000 species of native land snails, most of them very tiny. They are cousins to the sea snails. They are *gastropods*, which means they have one shell. They are also *pulmonates* because they have a lung, rather than gills.

- Most New Zealand snails are *dextrally* coiled. This means the spirals go clockwise from the centre. (The opposite is *sinistrally* coiled.)

- Snails have blue blood which does not clot. The oxygen-carrying pigment is *haemocyanin*, which is copper-based. Hence the blueness.

- Snails *hibernate* when it is very cold and *aestivate* when it is very dry. In both cases it is as if they are in a deep sleep. When conditions are right, they come back to life.

- Land snails are *hermaphrodites*. They have both male and female sex organs. When they mate, they swap little packets of sperm.

- There are three main groups of giant land snail in New Zealand: the *Placostylus* family, which includes the herbivorous flax snail; the *Poryphanta* family, which includes the giant kauri snail; and powelliphanta. Powelliphanta belong to the oldest family of carnivorous snails in the world. They mainly eat earthworms, slugs and soft-bodied invertebrates called springtails.

- Powelliphanta are named after Dr A.W.B. Powell, a former *conchologist* or shell and mollusc scientist at the Auckland Museum.

- Ancestors of powelliphanta were making their slimy way around New Zealand forests some 200 million years ago. They are great survivors.

- Most New Zealand powelliphanta are found in the lower North Island and upper South Island in cool high-altitude scrub zones. They like to live in deep, moist leaf mould.

- Powelliphanta lay a small number of dull-white eggs which look like birds' eggs and which come out of an opening near the snail's mouth! The eggs may not hatch for two to nine months. The small snails immediately take off on their own. Powelliphanta are slow growing and do not mature until they are 15 years old. Some live for 40 years or more.

- It is illegal to collect either live giant land snails or their shells. They are endangered because they are need moisture so much and their forest homes have been cleared. They are also eaten by wild pigs, rats and stoats and are trampled by cattle.

- SOS — 'Save Our Snails' is a group that cares for endangered invertebrates (not just snails) in any way they can. They plant flax and fence places where snails are found to keep them safe.

Giant giants

From treetop to forest floor, New Zealand is a land of ancient giants!

Pill millipedes defend themselves by rolling into a ball like a pill. New Zealand's giant pill millipede, *Procyliosoma tuberculata*, can reach 50 mm long and 25 mm wide. There are five species of pill millipede in New Zealand. They have 42 legs, not 1000.

The giant centipede, *Cormocephalus rubriceps*, can grow as long as 250 mm on a rat-free island. Centipedes have between 30 and 62 legs depending on the species, not 100.

Slugs are really just land snails without shells. The native veined leaf slugs, putoko ropiropi or *Athoracophorus bitentactulatus*, grow to 40 mm long, and are yellowish in colour with reddish-brown veins like a leaf.

The largest native earthworm, *Diporochaeta gigantea*, which is another passenger from Gondwana, reaches a massive 1.4 metres long and 11 mm wide. There are 173 native worm species.

Terry Black, a snail-search volunteer, looks as if he is swimming in a sea of scrub on Mount Taranaki.

9 Walking on wrists
Pekapeka tou poto, the short-tailed bat

SALLY BROWN WAS COOKING tea when she heard the swing of the cat door. She expected to feel Benjy's smooth body against her legs but nothing happened. She stopped and listened. There was pattering in the bathroom — something small and light was being tossed around.

'Oh, oh,' she thought. 'What now?'

She hurried to take a look. The cat was crouching beside the bathmat. It had been rucked up and there was a suspicious bulge in the middle.

'Benjy! What have you got?' she asked, picking up the mat. She screamed. 'Oh my God. What is *that*?'

The animal on the tiles had a body the size of a mouse but its legs were long and bony, it had tiny clawed feet, a small triangular face, large ears and a snout like a very small pig. Its open mouth showed two rows of tiny pointed teeth. It was covered in soft, slightly frosted red-tinted velvety fur. Between the forelegs and the animal's body there was a fine, thin membrane. It reminded her of an inside-out umbrella, a mess of snapped vanes and torn fabric. It was dead.

The cat purred proudly, his blue eyes shining.

NEW ZEALAND

PASSPORT
URUWHENUA

CLASS
Mammal

ORDER
Chiroptera

FAMILY
Mystacinidae

SCIENTIFIC NAME
Mystacina tuberculata

COMMON NAME
Short-tailed bat

MĀORI NAME
Pekāpekā tou poto

The first reports of bats near Rangataua came in the 1970s when a DOC worker found a dead one in the forest. It was noted but nothing else was done. Short-tailed bats are very small, they come out only after dark, and if you don't know where to look, they will not be found.

By 1993, however, when Benjy brought the bat home, everything had changed because a *bat detector* had been invented.

Bats do have eyes but sight is not much use in the dark, so they have an extra way of 'seeing' — they make loud squeaks that are beyond the range of human hearing, called *ultrasound*. Their large ears collect the echoes from the squeaks as they bounce off things, giving the bat a detailed and accurate picture of the world. Bat detectors translate the squeaks into clicks so humans can hear them.

Sally lived in the small settlement of Rangataua, near Rangataua Forest on the southern slopes of Mount Ruapehu. The 10,000-hectare forest is part of Tongariro National Park and so it has never been logged or burned. It contains many old red beech trees, some of them 40 metres high and more than two metres around. Some of the trees are thought to be over 400 years old.

One of the DOC rangers took a bat detector into the forest. It was clicking like a Geiger counter. 'Hello!' he thought. Up to a short time before, it was thought that short-tailed bats lived in only three places in New Zealand but now it seemed a significant colony of them had been found.

Brian Lloyd, who is a *chiroptologist* or bat scientist, went to Rangataua straight away. Since then, he has spent many hours on the mountain studying the bats. In particular, he came to know one rather slow little bat named Pluto very well. Brian named him Pluto because he reminded him of the comic-book character.

Around the end of December each year, female bats give birth to one baby. They have to go out to feed at night, so they do what some human mothers do — they carry their offspring to a crèche, a maternity tree, and pop back every so often to feed them. The crèche holds thousands of bat babies and in the squash and wriggle of that noisy crowded tree, Pluto fell out.

'Hello, little fella,' Brian said when he picked him up. 'What's wrong?' Pluto was nearly dead. He had been on the ground all night and had not been fed. He was cold and shivering. Brian took him home and his colleague, Shirley McQueen, nursed the little bat back to life. He could not go back to the colony so he became part of the family and when he grew up he became a bat-ambassador, visiting schools and marae with Brian.

'He was with us for about 18 months,' Brian says. 'He wasn't very bright. He used to wander around the kitchen floor and go into a corner and get stuck! He'd be sitting there echo-locating away — "Can't go that way, can't go that way" — and we'd pick him up and turn him around and he'd go, "Oh, oh, all right" and off he'd go for a couple of flights around the room. He was great.'

Pluto escaped not long after Brian moved house. He may have been caught by a cat or, as he was not far from his colony, perhaps he was able to find his way back there. Who knows, he might be having his say in the middle of all that squeaking, noisy colony right now.

Pluto, not long after he was found on the ground outside his roost. He was not too good!

Who's who in the maternity tree

How do the mothers know which bat baby is theirs? There may be many thousand batlets in the tree hollering 'Me! Me!' and yet the mothers are just like any mothers around the world. They know their little ones.

'Move over! Move over!' 'Keep still!' 'Stop pushing!' 'Be quiet!' Life inside a crowded house.

A cathedral in the forest

There are over 7000 short-tailed bats in Rangataua Forest. They spend the daytime roosting upside-down in about 30 different large red beeches which have been hollowed out over hundreds of years to make huge wooden chimneys with massive piles of bat dung outside — this is called 'guano', just like bird droppings.

One of the trees, which researchers have called 'Nôtre Dame' because it reminds them of the huge cathedral in Paris, can hold as many as 5500 bats. 'When they leave the tree at night, it takes 40 minutes. When you see them all come out — *Whooa!* That is really *something!*' says Brian. When they come back before dawn, they pack into a squeaking, wriggling mass, all arguing and grizzling about the lack of space.

The bats stay only a few days or weeks in each tree, possibly so that predators don't find them, but the main reason they have survived is that their forest is untouched. Short-tailed bats *must* have old trees.

In the name of science

Scientists have to do all sorts of things. One time Brian was studying the effects of *torpor* on bats. Torpor is like hibernation — the temperature drops or the bat runs out of energy so it just shuts down for a while. Brian had a room set up in his house, a *batarium*, with 20 bats in it. In order to induce torpor he would take the bats and put them in the fridge. Some of his mates accused him of being batty!

Tracking bats

Scientists use technology to learn things they would never have known 20 years ago. As well as being hand-held, bat detectors can be linked to voice-activated tape recorders left in the bush. Then, when bats fly past at night, the detectors switch on the tapes. Tiny transmitters, less than a gram in weight, can be attached to bats to find out where they go. Infra-red cameras make it possible to find out what goes on in the nests and beside the trees.

Bat detectors have helped find many more colonies of short-tailed bat. Some, such as the colonies in Te Urewera or Whirinaki, are huge in comparison with Rangataua. Others, such as those in the Tararua Ranges, are very small.

Bat facts

- There are more than 960 species of bat in the world. After rodents, they are the second biggest group of mammals. Most live in the tropics or subtropics. The smallest, the bumble-bee bat, weighs 2.5 grams and the largest, the flying fox, weighs 1.5 kg.

- New Zealand has — or had — three bat species, the only mammals here before humans. The long-tailed bat, *Chalinolobus tuberculatus*, is the most common, although it is still rare. It probably blew in from Australia a couple of million years ago. Like most bats, it comes out at dusk and feeds on insects which it catches in the air. As well as living in the bush, it has shown that it can survive in plantations and farmland.

  The other two are — or were — *something else*. The greater short-tailed bat, *Mystacina robusta*, became extinct in the 1960s when rats invaded the islands where they lived, leaving just the lesser short-tailed bat, *Mystacina tuberculata*. They are the only ones of their family in the world.

- About 86 million years ago, New Zealand was still part of Gondwana. It was joined to Antarctica, and Antarctica was joined to South America. There was no polar ice and the ancestors of the short-tailed bat gradually spread across the continent from South America. Then, like many of the creatures in this book, they were marooned when the land masses split.

  That was cool. Life here was relatively safe. Over the years, short-tailed bats became very terrestrial — they spend a lot of time on the land, not in the air like other bats. In order to do this, they have made an amazing adaptation — they have strong limbs, relatively large feet with strong claws, and a way of folding and protecting their wings so that the tips go into small pockets on the sides of their bodies. Then they walk on what would be their wrists — if they were human! They spend most of their time in the dark on tree trunks or the forest floor looking for fruit, nectar, pollen and insects.

- Short-tailed bats are *lek breeders*, like kakapo. At mating time, male bats fight to see who gets the best small hole in a tree and then they sing for up to 10 hours a night for about 12 weeks. ♪♪

  People can hear their high-pitched warble over 50 metres away. Each night, female bats visit the singing males to mate.

Another crowded house! These little animals don't believe in personal space.

A scientist went to the doctor.

'I've got a headache,' he said. 'It's because I live in the same room as two of my brothers. One of them has six goats and the other has four pigs and they all live in the room with us. The smell is terrible.'

'Couldn't you just open the windows?' asked the doctor.

'Certainly not,' the scientist replied, 'my bats would fly out.'

You can see the sharp little teeth, the large ears, the podgy feet, the piggy-like tail and the umbrella-like wing of this short-tailed bat from the Omahuta State Forest.

The bat fly on the back of this bat is found only in New Zealand. It has no close relative in the world. It feeds on bat guano, or bat droppings. It is distantly related to the fruit fly.

Bats and roses

Night video has been used to unravel the mystery of an amazing plant, the wood rose, *Dactylanthus taylorii*. It is New Zealand's only completely parasitic flowering plant, meaning that it lives completely off another plant. Its Maori name, 'pua-o-te-reinga', means 'flower of the underworld' because it is found on and under the bush floor. Like the bat, the rose needs healthy, diverse forests.

It is highly endangered.

For about three months of the year, the rose has large, fleshy, strongly scented male and female flowers which have to be pollinated for it to make seed. Scientists were puzzled. The plant made so much nectar they wondered which insect could be doing the pollination … You guessed it — when they videotaped the flowers and viewed the tapes, there was a short-tailed bat! It fluttered down and feasted on the nectar about 40 times in one night.

10 Stoatal enemies
Rowi, the Okarito brown kiwi

The kiwi . . . is doomed to final extinction . . . like the moa, the mammoth, and the mastadon, their use in creation has come to a close . . . It looks like a being one would expect to see in the moon, Mars, or some dying out Planet. When running about in the moonlight, it looks like the ghost of a bird . . .

— Charles Douglas,
Birds of South Westland, 1899

NEW ZEALAND
PASSPORT
URUWHENUA

CLASS
Aves

ORDER
Struthioniformes: ratites

FAMILY
Apterygidae: kiwi

MĀORI NAMES FOR DIFFERENT VARIETIES
Kiwi, roa, rowi, tokoeka

NO ONE SEES THE KILLER moving through the bush at nightfall, her nose and whiskers twitching, her eyes bright. She is chestnut-brown, soft and lithe, a stoat with five kittens waiting in her nest. Like them, she is beginning to starve.

Last year, there was a burst of rimu fruit. Rats bred in their thousands and life was good, but this year the rats have gone and she is desperate. She flows over and under fallen logs like a snake, until she comes to a recently cut track. She follows it along the bank of a small creek towards the hills.

The young rowi is just waking. He is only five months old but has been on his own for weeks, hiding in burrows by day, feeding by night.

He steps into damp forest leaves and searches for worms and grubs, sniffing and snorting as he plunges his long beak into the soft soil.

Suddenly he stops. His keen ears have heard the softest of sounds, a faint snap, but he is not sure where the danger is.

Five metres away, the stoat is confused. She can smell the rowi but there is something else — rat. She has come to a rectangular wooden box partly hidden by branches. Her nose twitches. She starts to salivate. There is a stoat-size hole at one end of the box — a tunnel. Her eyes gleam. *Stoats love tunnels.* She goes in.

Inside, the stench of decaying rat is overpowering. There's a stick lying sideways across the middle of the tunnel but she can see the rat shape on the other side. She lightly leaps over the stick and comes down on the spring-plate of a Fenn trap. There's a muffled bang as the steel jaws slam shut, breaking her back and killing her instantly.

The little rowi hears the bang and now he can smell the stoat. He hurries into his burrow and stays very still for a long time before coming out to feed again.

A kiwi is most likely to be killed in its first year. If it manages to survive that time between egg and adult, it is very likely to live another

The Fenn trap kills the stoat instantly.

Kiwi killers

Depending on species and locality, kiwi are threatened on a number of fronts. They have a strong scent which attracts dogs, and they are killed with one bite because they have no sternum and wing muscles to protect their lungs. In 1987 a dog killed 500 kiwi in Waitangi Forest in six weeks — that's half the birds that were there.

Ferrets are a problem, as are their smaller stoat cousins. In the 1980s ferret farming was popular and many were simply set free in the wild when the fashion for their fur ended. Big mistake!

Possums don't often kill kiwi but they *love* those rich large eggs. Sometimes kiwi are also caught in carelessly set possum traps or killed by cyanide bait.

Natural hazards include being beaten up by other kiwi! Kiwi are very territorial and defend an area of about 40 hectares. They call at each other and can be vicious with their sharp claws. When young kiwi are released at the end of Operation Nest Egg, care is taken not to put them where they will be killed by other kiwi.

Hazards created by humans are things like effluent ponds, cattle-stops and roads.

Kiwi have been completely protected since 1896.

30 or 40 years, able to defend itself against most enemies. Once it reaches the magic weight of 1 kg, it seems, it will be OK.

That is why Operation Nest Egg was started. In 1991, people realised with horror that the kiwi was in great danger. Kiwi numbers had fallen from around five million in the early 1920s, to around 80,000, a level and a trend that would see them extinct in the wild within decades.

The Kiwi Recovery Programme was started. It is a partnership between DOC, the Royal Forest and Bird Protection Society, and the Bank of New Zealand. First it found out how many birds were left and why their numbers were falling. It was soon clear the crunch time was the period between egg and young adult. Operation Nest Egg began.

At Okarito, a small settlement on the west coast of the South Island not far from Franz Josef Glacier, things were very bad indeed. Rowi are New Zealand's rarest variety of kiwi — their numbers were down from around 11,000 in 1923 to 130 in 1998. It wasn't that rowi were not breeding, just that they were not making it through that first year.

For five years Operation Nest Egg took eggs from the rowi's nests and incubated them. The young kiwi were then kept in a breeding centre until they were old enough to go to Motuara, a predator-free offshore island in the Marlborough Sounds. After a year there, and once they had reached the magic weight of 1 kg, they were set free again at Okarito.

In 2001 there was great celebration when Inka, one of the first Operation Nest Egg rowi, mated with a wild bird at Okarito and their chick Dawn was hatched.

Massey University students Ross Martin and Anna Grant change a radio transmitter on an Operation Nest Egg North Island brown kiwi chick, Tongariro Forest, 1998.

Kiwi are killed by a number of things but at Okarito the stoat is the worst. Phase two of the programme was to deal with them.

In early 2001, the largest stoat-control operation in the world began. Okarito Forest is 980 hectares of rugged rainforest. Tracks were cut and 1500 stoat tunnels, some with two traps inside, were put in place. It was a huge and expensive job.

At the beginning of February 2002, what were to have been the last 14 Motuara rowi came back to Okarito. By October, 28 rowi eggs had been counted in the forest. For the first time since Operation Nest Egg, they were going to stay there and it looked like a good year ahead.

But nature has the last word. Fourteen young kiwi from those 28 eggs were being monitored, but by early January 2003 DOC realised they had all been killed by stoats. In spite of the traps! In spite of over 1000 stoats and 2600 rats being caught!

The reason was the bumper crop of rimu fruit in 2002. The rat population had exploded and the stoats had followed. By 2003, they had simply overwhelmed the trapping programme.

But not all was lost. Five eggs were still to hatch, although they were hidden deep in holes where no one could reach them. DOC staff had to wait motionless outside the burrows for hours on end until the young rowi came out. It was tricky, but they did it and were able to transfer two young kiwi to Motuara. So, Operation Nest Egg continues. Luckily, no adult deaths were recorded. It was a bad year, but it's not expected to happen again. Charles Douglas' gloomy prediction of a century ago is *not* going to come true!

The battle to save kiwi is taking place all over New Zealand. Further south, Paul van Klink is checking Kahu, a Haast tokoeka chick, in the Haast Tokoeka Sanctuary, South Westland, 2002.

A little spotted kiwi chick on Kapiti Island.

Small but perfectly formed

No other creatures do it like this. Other birds have *chicks*. Chicks are bald or blind or fluffy — and, almost always, helpless. Their frantic parents care for them for months. Mammals have *babies*. They have big heads and small limbs and a lot of growing to do. Some, like humans, are cared for by their parents for years before they leave the nest.

Not kiwi. What astonishing birds! Instead of all that running around after their young when they are hatched — or born — kiwi pack everything their offspring need into one *huge* egg and let it all happen inside.

The kiwi egg is massive. It is one-fifth the size of the female bird. No wonder she hands everything over to the male once she has finished laying. He then sits on it for about *80 days*. He looks after the young when they hatch, guarding the entrance to the burrow.

When the kiwi chick emerges, it is a small but perfect copy of its parents. No messing around waiting to get feathers, grow wings or learn to walk. In a couple of weeks it is nearly ready to look after itself. If it were not for stoats and co., this would be a very good system!

The grey feathers and white patches of a rowi.

A great spotted kiwi at Mount Bruce.

A North Island brown kiwi at Rotorua.

Kiwi facts

- Kiwi evolved around 70 million years ago. They are *ratites*, flightless birds with flat breastbones. There are 11 living species of ratite, including emus, cassowaries, ostriches and rheas. On the other hand, there are nearly 10,000 species of *carinates*, birds which fly and have keels on their breastbones to attach flight muscles.

- Ratites have strong legs and reduced wings. They don't have strongly vaned flight feathers. A very long time ago, all ratites had a shared flying ancestor.

- Kiwi kai is earthworms, spiders, fallen fruit and seeds, insects and invertebrates. They have been known to kill and eat eels and frogs.

- There are six 'varieties' of kiwi. When research into genetics and blood typing is complete, it is likely that those varieties will be named as separate species. They weigh between 1 and 3.5 kg, depending on species and sex. Their large and muscular legs make up a third of that. They have four toes.

The *little spotted kiwi* is the smallest. It has a pleasant personality. Perhaps because it is not so aggressive and because of its size, it has become extinct on the mainland apart from places like the Karori Wildlife Sanctuary in Wellington. Kapiti Island is a stronghold for little spotted kiwi.

The *great spotted kiwi* lives in the South Island only. It is big, bold and handsome.

The *North Island brown kiwi* is tough! It is known for being stroppy and bad-tempered. It is found in the upper North Island.

The *rowi* or *Okarito brown kiwi* was only identified as a different variety in 1993. It has greyish feathers and sometimes has white patches on its head.

The *southern tokoeka* is short, round and bigger than the brown kiwi. It is found in Fiordland and on Stewart Island. It is more communal than the others.

The *Haast tokoeka* is found in the rugged areas behind Haast in the South Island.

Dogs Olly (left) and Lucy have been helping Rogan Colbourne track down a juvenile southern tokoeka on Stewart Island.

Bird or mammal?

'Incredible!' 'You're joking!' That's what they said when the first kiwi was taken to London in the 1830s. This creature from the other side of the world just did not seem possible. A number of animals in this book have been described as being like mammals — the mouse-like Stephens Island wren, or the monkey-like kokako. But none comes anywhere near the kiwi for having a bet both ways.

Kiwi are definitely birds, no doubt about it — beaks, eggs, wings, feathers. But they also have mammal-like features that make them 'the strangest of all living birds'.

Kiwi have a lower body temperature than most birds, and a metabolic rate more like that of a mammal. Kiwi bones contain marrow, not air sacs. The male has a well-developed penis and the female has two ovaries, whereas most male birds don't have much of a penis and females only have one ovary — it's less weight when they are flying.

Most birds have keen eyesight but poor smell and hearing but kiwi have an excellent sense of smell and quite large earholes. They sometimes listen with their heads on one side, or hold their beaks up like dogs as they sniff the wind. Their nostrils are at the *end* of their beaks rather than the top.

Kiwi have feathers like hair, whiskers like a cat, and no tail feathers. They can't fly. Their wings are tiny and have a small claw at the end. And they live in burrows, like badgers, with some species having one-entrance holes, and others having elaborate tunnel-and-den systems.

It's no wonder those Londoners were astonished!

Tane's hidden bird

Tane, god and creator of the forest, loved kiwi. They were the first birds created, the big sisters and brothers of humans, but most of all, he loved them after they made their great sacrifice.

It happened a very long time ago. The forest was dying from bugs that were drilling and munching and destroying the trees. Tane called the birds and lined them up in front of him. In those days, they all had wings and lived in the tree-tops.

'I need one pair of you to go down to the forest floor and kill these bugs,' Tane said. 'Who will do this job for me?'

One by one, the birds made excuses. Tui were afraid, pukeko did not want to wet their feet, and pipiwharauroa (shining cuckoo) were nest-building. At last, the kiwi hopped forward. 'We will go,' they said.

They had to lose their beautiful wings and leave the light and the sun. They had to learn to live in burrows in the ground, to come out at night when the bugs were feeding, and never again fly through blue skies. Their beaks grew long and thin and they sprouted whiskers. Their bright flying feathers became hairy and brown and their feet became huge.

In return, kiwi became the most famous and well-loved birds of all. But as for the others — well, tui wear the coward's white feather, pukeko have wet feet forever and pipiwharauroa have never ever built a nest again.

Pipiwharauroa, the shining cuckoo. The proud home-maker would never again build a nest.

11 Oh, corker! Corker! Corker!
Toutouwai pango, the black robin

IN 1976 THE BLACK ROBIN was the world's rarest bird. There were only seven left. Although no one knew it at the time, if the female named Old Blue had died, that would have been the end of the story and another name on New Zealand's list of extinct birds.

For over 100 years, the tiny birds had clung to existence. They lived on Little Mangere Island in the Chatham Islands. It was an unfriendly stump of rock surrounded by 200-metre-high cliffs. There had once been bush on the top of the island but for a long time it had been slowly dying. Muttonbirds had weakened the trees by burrowing, and the smothering muehlenbeckia vine was moving in. The final blow was when a helicopter pad was constructed so people could harvest the muttonbirds. It opened up the bush that remained and the wind roared in.

In 1972, there had been 18 birds left, but just five breeding pairs.

By 1976 there were seven and only two of them were females. Nothing could be done to Little Mangere in time to rescue the birds. It was time for the Wildlife Service to consider moving them.

Mangere Island is 100 metres from Little Mangere. It is bigger than Little Mangere, with a similar amount of bush, but since sheep had been removed in 1968 it was in much better condition.

Moving the birds was an extraordinary operation. It wasn't just that seven wildlife officers had to catch the birds and then descend the 200-metre cliffs on ropes — a journey that took an hour over crumbling lichen-encrusted rock, with the sea below. It was also that it was then extremely difficult to land on Mangere, where large, greasy boulders are washed by a big surf.

Luck was on the wildlife team's side. No one drowned. No legs were broken. No birds were lost. As the first newly released robin flew into the bush, Tony Billing, one of the officers, could not stop himself. He exclaimed, 'Oh, corker! Corker! Corker!' — and that became a theme of the black robin rescue programme whenever something good happened.

NEW ZEALAND
PASSPORT
URUWHENUA

CLASS
Aves

ORDER
Passeriformes: perching birds

FAMILY
Muscicapidae: warblers, thrushes and allies

SCIENTIFIC NAME
Petroica traversi

MĀORI NAME
Toutouwai pango

That was just the beginning. The next years were like walking a tightrope. By 1978 two more birds had died and there were only five black robins. In 1979, there were *still* only five black robins, but a different five, as one had hatched but one had died.

Don Merton of the Wildlife Service made a daring proposal. He suggested something that had never been done before. It was a

Black robin facts

- Black robins have been in the Chatham Islands a long time. Their ancestors are believed to have flown from Australia via the New Zealand mainland thousands of years ago. In their time on the Chathams their feathers have turned black, their legs have grown longer, and though they can still fly a little, they have begun to spend more time on the ground.

- Black robins can live to be 6–13 years old. Old Blue died at the age of 13, much later than was expected. It was a good thing she lived that long. All the black robins living today are descended from her and her mate Old Yellow. This is not ideal as it means there is no genetic variability in the population but we are lucky to have any black robins at all.

- Black robins grow to 150 mm. They eat insects such as cockroaches and weta, as well as grubs and worms, and spend a lot of time on or near the forest floor.

- Black robins begin to breed at around two years. They often stay with their mates for life. They like to make their nests in hollow trees or stumps, but if there are none of those they will nest in the branches of trees. They will chase other black robins away from their areas. Females usually lay two eggs. The male looks after the female by feeding her and singing to her while she sits on the eggs. Both parents feed the chicks in the nest and afterwards, until they are about 65 days old.

gamble but the robins were not breeding quickly enough. At any time, a disaster could wipe them out.

Robins will lay a second clutch of eggs if they lose the first set — and then a third if those are lost. And some birds will incubate and raise the chicks of other birds — as the cuckoo knows.

It was risky, but the Wildlife Service team would try it. Eggs were taken from the robins' nests and placed in the nests of the Chatham Island warblers. At first it seemed to work — the eggs hatched and the warblers began to feed them. Then, a black robin chick died at 10 days old. The warblers had not been able to feed it enough.

The team turned to another bird, the Chatham Island tomtit. It is small and friendly — a good choice. Only problem was, there were none on Mangere. They were on *another* island — South East Island. There was nothing for it but to carry the eggs there, a bumpy hour's boat-ride away.

This time, the fostering worked. There was still a lot more to be done, including back-fostering to stop young black robins growing up thinking they were tomtits, but today there are 250 black robins.

They now live mainly on South East Island, which has more space for them, and there are still some on Mangere. And the bush is recovering on their original home, Little Mangere, so perhaps one day they will be returned there.

Corker! Corker! Corker!

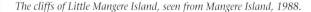

The cliffs of Little Mangere Island, seen from Mangere Island, 1988.

A black robin chick being transferred from nest to nest, South East Island, 1984.

The Chatham Island tomtit foster parent feeds two black robin fledglings on South East Island in the Chatham Islands, December 1985.

Derek Brown transfers a black robin egg into a Chatham Island tomtit foster nest, 1987.

Man meets bird! Rick Thorpe and a Chatham Island tomtit in its nest box eye each other on South East Island, 1987. The tomtit is a black robin foster parents and Rick is checking that all is well.

The landing party climbs the cliffs of Little Mangere Island to take the black robins to their new home on Mangere Island in October 1976.

Old Blue, the female Chatham Island black robin that laid the eggs that saved her species.

Another home for the black robin

By 2002, the black robin breeding programme had been so successful that South East Island and Mangere Island were crowded. Breeding had slowed and many black robins raised each spring were dying because of lack of space.

DOC looked for a new home for them. They decided to try a fenced, predator-free 35-hectare block called Caravan Bush (left) on nearby Pitt Island. Fourteen black robins were released.

DOC knew this was risky, because although they could fence predators out, they could not fence the black robins in. And sadly, that is what happened. The birds flew out of their safe area and by early 2003 all but one were thought to be dead — they had probably been eaten by cats.

There are not many more safe places in the Chatham Islands but it is not likely that the Chatham Islands iwi will allow the black robins to be moved to other parts of New Zealand, so DOC plans to try again on Pitt Island. The fight for the black robin continues.

Pitt Island schoolchildren help release the 14 Chatham Island black robins at Caravan Bush on the island in September 2002.

Cross-fostering cuckoo-style
— the mohoua and its large house guest

Don Merton and DOC are not the only ones to make use of the generous nature of some of New Zealand's small birds. The cuckoo has known about cross-fostering ever since Tane punished it for not going down to the forest floor to eat bugs (see p. 73).

The grey warbler and its Chatham Island cousin both regularly bring up the offspring of the pipiwharauroa (shining cuckoo), which happily lays its eggs in the warbler's nest then flies to the Pacific for the summer.

A similar thing happens with the long-tailed cuckoo and three other insect-eating birds. The long-tailed cuckoo lays its eggs in whitehead nests in the North Island and in the nests of their cousins the brown creeper and the yellowhead, or mohoua, in the South Island.

Mohoua (*Mohoua ochrocephala*) are classed as endangered. Not because of the cuckoo, although that probably doesn't help — and what will happen to the cuckoo if mohoua disappear?

In the 1930s mohoua were described as the second most common bird in the South Island after the koromiko (bellbird), but they are now in steep decline. This small, round-headed, bright-coloured bird lives in beech forests where it eats insects and can sometimes be seen flocking in noisy groups. Like many other birds in this book, it nests in holes in trees. It also has a long incubation and nesting time, all of which means it is easy pickings for stoats and rats. Same old story.

Peter Dilks climbing to check mohoua nest boxes in the Eglinton Valley, 1996.

A mohoua brings home the grub.

That's a long-tailed cuckoo on the top left of the page, and left, two mohoua are outside the hole where they are nesting.

When push comes to shove
The weta with horns

IT IS A VERY DARK NIGHT. It has been raining and the sky is full of racing clouds. When they part the moon shines through, but it is a weak, slender thing. There is barely enough light to show the silent shapes of the nearby islands or the white caps of the waves.

This is Atiu, or Middle Mercury Island, off the east coast of Coromandel Peninsula. It is long and thin and rises sharply from the sea. Tall cliffs on three sides are hung with pohutukawa. Along the central spine there is thick bush. It is only 13 hectares, little more than a rock in the sea. It is a wildlife sanctuary and landing here is not permitted. For thousands of years, Atiu has been much the same. There are no introduced mammals — no rats, stoats, cats, dogs, possums or hedgehogs.

The moon disappears and the dark returns.

It is a signal.

In the centre of the island, in a hollow under trees where the ground is soft and leaf-covered, a small trapdoor lid made of spit and soil is lifted aside to show the shaded shape of a burrow. Two long antennae appear. They delicately feel the air. *Is anything there?*

Two legs follow, then rest a moment, listening. *Listening?* Yes. This is Motu, the tusked weta! Like most of his kind, his ears, all four of them, are just beside his knees on his front legs.

Next come two brown polished horns and a shiny brown head with black-button eyes. Motu can't see with them as we do, but he can tell it's good and dark. The best time for weta.

All clear! He scrambles from his tunnel. It is several days since he has eaten and he fancies an earthworm or beetle. He moves carefully across the hollow, his antennae before him, his palps testing the air.

He is a handsome specimen, a young adult with a fine set of curved brown tusks and thick armour-plating. He has long hind legs covered in spines.

'Tsit-tsit!'

It is the sound of another weta. Close. In his territory! An intruder! He is instantly alert and raises his hind legs in reply, striking them hard against his body. 'TSIT-TSIT!'

There is an answering rasp as the intruder rattles his tusks. They charge. *WHAM!* They lock horns. Push! Shove! *Nnngh!* Head to head! The hollow fills with the sound of 12 legs paddling desperately in the damp leaves. Round and round they spin, backwards and forwards.

Motu is slowly losing but he will not give in. Then suddenly his hind leg finds a rock to push against. It is all he needs! *NNNNGHH!* The challenger weakens and begins to back away. Motu charges and

NEW ZEALAND
PASSPORT
URUWHENUA

PHYLUM
Arthropoda

CLASS
Insect

ORDER
Orthoptera

FAMILY
Anostostomatidae

SCIENTIFIC NAME
Motuweta isolata

COMMON NAMES
Mercury Island tusked weta, elephant weta, Middle Island monster

MĀORI NAME
Motuweta

Atiu, or Middle Mercury Island.

twists his head, flipping his foe onto his back. For a moment the challenger lies helplessly waving his legs, then he wriggles to his feet. In an instant, he is gone.

Tuatara has been sleeping all day on a rock not far from the hollow and is also hungry. Now that the rain has stopped, she wanders into the trees. It is too dark to see but she knows what the rustling, the bony crack of small horns and the *TSIT! TSIT!* of fighting weta means. She flicks her tongue.

At that moment the clouds blow apart and she can see. A weta is very close and looking the other way. She lumbers towards it, her jaws wide. A fraction of a second from death, Motu senses danger and his powerful hind legs react. With one spring he launches himself. *Boinng!* He flies a metre into the air, onto a log and out of sight in the leaves.

The dark closes in again.

Tuatara yawns. Too bad.

Until 1970, no one knew tusked weta existed. One day a scientist named Tony Whitaker, who was studying lizards on Atiu, found a weta that did not look like anything he had ever seen. It was large and had tusks or horns — like a bull or an elephant, which is why it is sometimes called the 'elephant weta'. It was one of the most exciting scientific discoveries of the 20th century — as exciting as finding the kakapo!

Since then, two more lots of tusked weta have been found, one in Northland and another in Raukumara in the East Cape region.

Tusked weta can measure up to 90 mm. Only the males have tusks, but the females are about the same length because they have long, egg-laying tails called *ovipositors*. The ovipositors look a bit like stings, but unless you fear being hit by an egg, it's not this end of the weta you should look out for.

Dead as . . .

'Dead as a dodo' and 'dumb as a dodo' are both sayings but only the first one is true! The dodo was like many New Zealand creatures: it lived so long in safety on its island of Mauritius that it became a trusting, flightless giant. It didn't stand a chance when European sailors found it — what they didn't kill for food and fun, their dogs and pigs did. In 80 years the dodos were all gone.

When a species is only found in one place, then it is in great danger. If anything happens, like a sudden disease or fire, it will be *dead as a dodo*.

Tusked weta are seriously endangered and there were so few of them that DOC had to act. Tusked weta were so precious that DOC practised breeding and moving a non-endangered species first. When they were sure it would be safe, they shifted some of the Atiu tusked weta to Landcare Research at Mt Albert in Auckland and some to Auckland Zoo.

It was a major conservation effort and it took about five years but it was a great success. In 2000, at the end of the project, 100 young tusked weta were released on islands not far from Atiu, on Moturehu and Whakau and they have since bred there.

Paul Barrett is the *entomologist*, or insect specialist, who was in charge of the breeding programme at Auckland Zoo. He welcomed the chance to study tusked weta and found them smarter than you might think. For instance, he noticed that female tusked weta didn't make their burrows near their food trays as he had expected. Instead, they made them where they wanted them. Then, in the dark of night, they lifted the lids of their burrows, came out and carried the food trays over to them.

When he moved the food trays back again, the same thing happened! They were modifying their world to suit themselves.

He also found that the tusked weta are almost entirely carnivorous. They will not only eat baby mice with gusto, they are not fussy about eating each other if they are left together too long!

'They have very sharp mandibles and eat any prey up to the size of themselves that can't get away,' Paul says. 'If they were very large, we'd need to worry . . .'

Mercury Islands

The seven islands in the Mercury Group lie about 8 km east of the Coromandel Peninsula. In order of size they are Ahuahu (Great Mercury Island), Whakau (Red Mercury Island), Kawhitu (Stanley Island), Moturehu (Double Island), Atiu (Middle Island), Korapuki and Green Island.

All but Ahuahu are wildlife sanctuaries so you must have a DOC permit to land on them.

Atiu has no introduced predators, but it does have tuatara, several species of large skinks, New Zealand's largest gecko, and giant centipedes — and they are all hunters of tusked weta.

Weta facts

- Weta are *orthoptera*, which means they belong to the same order as grasshoppers and crickets. They are flightless and have powerful, enlarged hind legs that some species use to make their *tsit-tsit* call. They are all nocturnal. By day they shelter in holes in logs and trees or in tunnels and spaces under stones and in the ground.

- There are more than 100 species of weta in New Zealand, in five groups: tree weta, ground weta, cave weta, giant weta and tusked weta.

  The *tree weta* is the one you are most likely to find in your gumboot. You can identify the male by his large head. Tree weta are survivors.

  Ground weta are small and don't have ears or make sounds. Like tusked weta, they live in holes in the ground. There are 36 species of them.

  Cave weta also don't have ears. Their legs are very long and their bodies are short. There are 60 species of them.

  Giant weta and *tusked weta* are so spectacular they get stories of their own. (See the giant weta story on the next page.)

- Weta are tough! They can live on the highest mountains, near the seashore, and in all places in between. Mountain rock weta live above the snowline: they freeze solid in winter and thaw back to life in spring. How they do it is a mystery. *No antifreeze!*

- Weta have many traditional enemies such as cold-blooded tuatara, skinks and geckos, as well as birds like kiwi. However, they also have mammalian enemies like rats, stoats and cats, which are warm-blooded. Being warm-blooded means they need more food to eat, and also that they are very much better at finding it!

  That is why many weta which once lived on the mainland are now found only on offshore islands. Their homes have been destroyed or changed or they have been eaten to death — or both. The good news is that weta respond to care and attention. They breed easily in captivity, can live in small areas and happily settle down in new homes — as long as they are free of those predators.

- Unfortunately, the droppings of adult weta contain a sex-scent called a pheromone. This is not only a come-one for other weta, it's a great advertisement for keen-nosed weta predators.

- Tusked weta are very large but they are not classed as giant weta — they are more like a kind of ground weta. They are mainly carnivorous and eat earthworms, beetles and caterpillars.

- Tusked weta die of old age after about three years. For the first two, they grow from eggs to adults. They shed their skins 10 times and each time they grow a little larger. Shedding skin is dangerous and happens only on the darkest nights — being caught with your skin half off is like being caught with your trousers down!

- In their last year, tusked weta mate many times. Females lay about 300 eggs in batches of three or four in the soil. Depending on the weather and the time of year, it might be some months before the eggs hatch. By then the parents may be dead but it doesn't matter, because there are now more weta nymphs ready to begin their journey to adulthood.

Weta were the rodents of pre-human New Zealand. They are a similar size to mice, are active at night, rest during the day and eat much the same things as rodents. Even their droppings are alike! Weta poos have rounded ends but rodent droppings are pointed.

Giant weta

The scientific name for giant weta, *Deinacrida*, means 'demon grasshopper'. This group of 11 species of weta are something else! They are huge! The largest-ever weighed in at 71 grams, a little more than a size-7 egg.

Deinacrida are thought to have the most ancient weta lineage in New Zealand. Their ancestors, which looked much as they do today, shared the world of the dinosaur 190 million years ago.

They are rather docile vegetarians and mostly exist only on offshore islands. However, one little group of them has its own mainland island. The Mahoenui giant weta were first found on a King Country farm in 1962, living in their special 160-hectare island of thick, prickly, old man gorse. It is a perfect shelter for them because rats and their mates don't like it.

Another giant, wetapunga, is the largest and heaviest of the giant weta. 'Wetapunga' is Maori for the god of ugly things. Maybe because things would get a bit ugly if you met one when you were climbing a tree! They live on Little Barrier Island, the only safe place for them.

Since 1980 it has been against the law to move, capture or hurt giant weta.

A volunteer on Mana Island shows how harmless a Stephens Island giant weta can be.

Wetaphobes / wetaphiles

Wetaphobes are people who are scared of weta. It is true that when they are cornered or handled badly, weta can bite. But *wetaphiles*, people who like weta, know that they're much smaller than people and that if they are handled correctly, they won't hurt anyone.

If you find a weta in your house, just carefully scoop it up inside a small towel. Then put the open towel outside under a bush so the weta can wander off in its own good time.

The people of the King Country are so proud of their giant weta that they have placed statues of them at one end of the town of Te Kuiti.

13 Turf wars on Tiri
Aroha, the one-tough takahe

THE ISLAND OF TIRITIRI MATANGI, the wildlife sanctuary in the Hauraki Gulf, covers 220 hectares. Heaps of space, you would think, for 19 or so takahe. Trouble is, takahe are clever, adaptable birds. They know a good spot when they see one, and as far as Aroha is concerned, the only place to be is on the grass outside the rangers' house beside the lighthouse.

And that's what led to the Battle of Coronary Hill. It very nearly killed her.

NEW ZEALAND
PASSPORT
URUWHENUA

CLASS
Aves

ORDER
Gruiformes: cranes, rails and allies

FAMILY
Rallidae: rails

SCIENTIFIC NAME
Porphyrio mantelli hochstetteri

COMMON NAME
Pass bird

PREVIOUS NAME
Notornis

MĀORI NAMES
Takahē, takahea, moho

The first takahe males, Mr Blue and Stormy, were moved to Tiri from Te Hoiere (Maud Island) in the Marlborough Sounds in 1991. The first female, JJ, arrived about a year later, and it wasn't long before JJ and Stormy were the proud parents of a chick — Aroha. Aroha was not big but she was tough and she was a survivor.

When she matured, she paired off with Mr Blue and in 1994 they brooded another of JJ's eggs and raised a male chick, Whetu.

Things were sweet for Aroha. She had two males in her life — her mate, Mr Blue, and her brother and foster chick, Whetu. They were the Lighthouse Gang and other takahe better look out, because they had a patch and they were going to defend it!

Then along came Kaitiaki. Kaitiaki is a large male from Kapiti Island. He tried to join them.

'He would never have been able to join except that Mr Blue had problems with his leg,' says Barbara Walter, one of the DOC rangers on Tiri. 'He was able to wheedle his way in. So then Aroha had *three* males in her life.'

All this time, JJ and Stormy, Aroha's parents, were living further down the road. But things were not well between them. JJ was unsettled.

On the day of the battle, Aroha and the Lighthouse Gang were grazing on Coronary Hill, when Aroha looked up to see JJ approaching. She was heading straight for her and she wanted her *outtathere*, no doubt about it. But Aroha was staunch. She wasn't going to be pushed around. She was going *nowhere!*

'There was a *huge* battle,' Barbara says.

When takahe fight, their razor-sharp secateur-beaks and heavy raking legs make a mighty mess. There's nipping and slashing and feathers flying. Bruises and black eyes and, sometimes, bodies.

Aroha lost.

She was very sorry for herself.

'She ended up right down behind the bunkhouse,' Barbara says. 'For a month we thought she might not live, she'd been beaten up so badly.'

But in time, small, spunky, stroppy Aroha mended, although she was never allowed to return to her old patch. JJ is the new boss of the Lighthouse Gang, and she makes it clear that Aroha is not welcome. Once a takahe has left and another has taken its place, that's it. No backs.

That was the end of Stormy, too. He became very stressed once JJ went. He grew thin and straggly and then, 'Suddenly one day he disappeared,' Barbara says.

In time, Aroha paired up with another male, Glencoe, and they made their home down the road. In 2002 Aroha and Glencoe produced their first chick, BJ, and again, in 2003, they had another. But Aroha has never accepted that she is not top of the pecking order, and that continues to cause problems — *bad*, *fatal* problems.

'She still thinks her territory is inside the gate,' Barbara says. 'So we have this ongoing battle.' In 2002, that led to BJ's death. He was chased and bowled by the Lighthouse Gang and died soon after.

'That could happen again this year because Aroha will not give up,' Barbara says. She sighs. It's a challenge, keeping these quarrelsome birds apart. But it's all worth it. She loves them, and she loves Aroha.

'You just have to admire her,' she says. 'She is *tough*.'

A juvenile takahe on Tiritiri Matangi.

Takahe are listed in the top ten endangered birds in the world. They are so rare that they were only seen *four times* in the 1800s and by the 1920s they were thought to be extinct.

Luckily, that was not so.

As a boy in Dunedin, Geoffrey Orbell was fascinated by the story of the missing bird which was then called 'Notornis'. As a young man, he saw the stuffed female takahe in Otago Museum which people thought had been the last one living — it had been killed in 1898 by Rough, a camper's dog.

When Orbell grew up and became a doctor in Dunedin, he and his mates spent weekends and holidays tramping in Fiordland. Now and then they heard of large bird prints on lake shores and of an enormous blue bird. *Was it the takahe?*

They began to search seriously.

On 11 April 1948 they explored an area of the Murchison Mountains beside Lake Te Anau. They climbed for four hours up a steep hillside and found themselves on a high cliff overlooking a deep valley. In the middle of the valley was a large lake which has since been named Lake Orbell. Later that day they saw tracks beside the lake which Orbell knew belonged to takahe. 'There you are, my boys,' he said. 'We've found him!'

On 20 November they returned. It was not long before they came across a large blue-green bird and its mate beside the lake. They captured, photographed and released them. 'The long search was over,' Orbell said. 'The Notornis wasn't extinct!'

Takahe country: these photographs were taken in the Murchison Mountains in the 1970s.

At the time it was estimated that there was a small but healthy population of around 500 takahe in the Murchison area. In 1953, a 500-square-km out-of-bounds area in Fiordland National Park was set aside just for them. It was thought that this might be enough to keep the takahe safe, but as the years went by it became clear that the birds in the park were not being replaced as they grew older and died. Chicks were hatched but not living to be adults. Numbers were plummeting.

By 1982 there were 118 known birds and it was time for emergency action. Three things happened.

First, because takahe often hatch two healthy eggs but raise only one chick, 'spare' fertile eggs were cross-fostered into the nests of infertile birds. Second, a takahe breeding unit was built at Burwood Bush near Te Anau. This meant eggs could be safely incubated and hatched, the young birds raised, then released to boost the wild population. Finally, some captive-bred birds from Burwood were taken to islands elsewhere — to Te Hoiere, Mana, Kapiti and Tiritiri Matangi. At least there will be breeding pairs in these places if anything happens to the Murchison takahe.

A takahe stripping seeds from mid-ribbed snow tussock in the Te Anau area.

Burwood Bush Captive Breeding Unit

Burwood opened in 1985. It works in much the same way as the kaki-raising programme at Twizel. 'Spare' eggs from wild takahe as well as eggs from the five breeding pairs at Burwood are incubated and hatched. Chicks are raised in brooder rooms, with dummy parents with heat pads for tummies and speakers for broadcasting takahe calls. The young birds are kept away from humans as much as possible and are even given lessons in recognising and attacking stoats!

From 1987 to 1999, 154 young takahe were sent from Burwood Bush back to the mountains and the islands.

A takahe embryo and egg in November 1957. This was the first attempt to rear takahe in captivity.

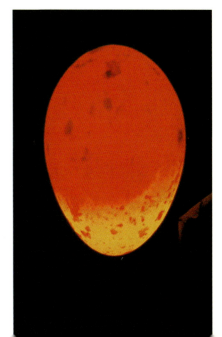

Left: A takahe chick being fed by a puppet at Burwood Bush.

Below left: A young adult takahe is having a transmitter attached so it can be tracked when it is released.

Below: A candled egg shows the age of the embryo inside and whether it is still healthy.

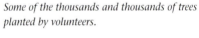

Tiritiri Matangi Island: A special place

Tiritiri Matangi has a long history of occupation. The first Maori were people of the Kawerau-a-Maki tribe, and later Ngati Paoa lived there. The island was purchased by Europeans in the 1830s and was cleared of bush and farmed from the 1850s.

In the early 1980s it became a scientific reserve. Between 1984 and 1994, 300,000 trees were planted by volunteers. It now has its own native plant nursery.

The Tiritiri Matangi lighthouse used to be famous for its brightness. In 1984 it was automated and downsized and the lighthouse keepers, Barbara and Ray Walter, began new careers as DOC rangers. Today, they and their team of assistants and volunteers look after the most diverse range of endangered species in any one place in New Zealand. (Read the list at www.tiritirimatangi.org.nz)

The island is unusual because it is a scientific reserve but it is also open to the public. Around 32,000 people visit every year and enjoy seeing and hearing how the bush once was, alive with movement and ringing with songs, calls and whistles. *It's magic!*

This is Blakie, having a splash and a drink not far from the lighthouse. Someone has fed on the sign.

Some of the thousands and thousands of trees planted by volunteers.

The Lighthouse Gang. Visitors are astonished to see some of the rarest birds in the world wandering on the grass like a bunch of blue chooks.

Takahe facts

- Takahe are the largest living members of the same family as pukeko and weka. They can grow to 500 mm and weigh over 3 kg. They have stocky bodies and short, rounded wings which they use for courtship and to show aggression. Their feathers are very soft because they are used only to keep warm — not for flying. They have extremely strong beaks with a red shield above them. Takahe usually mate for life and share the incubation of eggs and the rearing of young.

- Male and female takahe look alike, which has caused interesting mix-ups! When Blossom was sent from Te Hoiere to Tiri, they thought he was a *she*. The same thing happened with Kaitiaki, from Kapiti.

- Takahe have a low reproductive rate. They live for over 20 years in captivity but less in the wild. They mostly do not breed until they are three years old. They lay one clutch of two or three eggs but, if that fails, may lay another lot. Usually only one chick makes it through the first winter.

- The chicks are black and fluffy and slowly change colour as they grow. They may stay with their parents for 18 months and sometimes help with the next season's chicks. Then *that's it kid! Move out!*

- The takahe in Fiordland live in the mountain tops in the warmer parts of the year. They eat one type of mountain daisy and the juicy lower stems of three kinds of tussock. When snow is thick in winter they move down into the bush where they eat the starchy roots of the summer green fern, *Hypolepus millefolium*.

This limited diet is a problem for the takahe. In the 1940s and 1950s red deer invaded Fiordland, eating and damaging the tussock, and leaving the takahe short of good food.

Stoats are also thought likely to be a problem. Adult takahe are stroppy enough to look after themselves and have even been known to kill a stoat, but chicks are very vulnerable. Despite their excellent camouflage in tussock, takahe nests are easily sniffed out by hungry hunters.

Shooting deer and trapping stoats are helping save takahe.

- The population in August 2002 was 242 — a long way to go yet.

Tarkapoos! If you eat snow tussock, it shows in your droppings.

The fabulous feathers of a takahe.

Takahe? Pukeko?

Many millions of years ago, a bird that looked much like the pukeko flew to New Zealand. Food was plentiful and it had few enemies. Life was easy. In time its offspring became large and lost the power of flight.

Meanwhile, in Australia, pukeko remained much the same — they stayed small and could still fly. A few thousand years ago, some of these birds made their way to New Zealand and immediately settled in.

The similarity between takahe and pukeko is recognised in their scientific names. Pukeko are *Porphyrio porphyrio melantonus*, and takahe are *Porphyrio mantelli hochstetteri*. For quite a long time, takahe were called 'Notornis', which means 'southern bird'. The British taxonomist Richard Owen gave them this name because he thought they were sufficiently different from pukeko to be in a group of their own. In time, it was realised that they were related, so 'Notornis' was replaced.

Just to make things more complicated, there is another subspecies of takahe, *Porphyrio mantelli mantelli* — the North Island takahe. But they really *are* extinct.

14 Of holes & honey
The riddle of hihi, the stitchbird

THIS IS KAPITI ISLAND. It is 5 km off the south-west coast of the North Island. A storm has risen overnight and the cliffs on its western side are lashed by wind and high waves. At daybreak the high peak Tuteremoana is hidden by cloud. The rain is sharp and cold.

Ben Barr stands on the hut veranda in his waterproofs. He has waited as long as possible but now there's nothing for it. He grabs his gear and steps out. Hungry birds will be waiting.

Ben is a DOC contractor, working on Kapiti over the summer. He is looking after hihi, or stitchbirds. Ben's job is to make sure they are OK, locate and identify their nests, and catch and band fledglings. It's not easy because the nests are often very high, and hidden deep inside old hinau, kamahi pukatea, and sometimes, rata trees. Ben also looks after seven feeding stations on the island.

Hihi live in three main areas, called 'catchments', on the eastern side of Kapiti. Ben heads for the Te Rere catchment, a deep sheltered gully with several waterfalls. In the 1840s, much of the island was cleared by fire but Te Rere escaped. Some of the trees here are heavy and old, twisted and full of cracks and holes.

One is an ancient tree fuchsia. Each spring its orange-brown peeling-papery branches are covered in waxy purple, green and red flowers and later, with tasty black berries. It's the place to eat.

This morning it trembles as two hihi give it the once-over. They are not much larger than sparrows. She is well camouflaged, an olive brown-grey with white wing bars but he is a stand-out, with a smart velvet-black head, wicked white ear tufts, a white bar on his wing and bright golden shoulders. They both have whiskers, large brown eyes and perky tails which they often hold upward.

Despite the rain, they hop from one branch to the next, their narrow black bills reaching deep into the throats of the flowers for nectar. Their faces are covered in a dusting of bright blue pollen.

'*THRRRT!*' There is a furious flurry of wings. It is a tui. She wants this tree and she wants it now and there is no way she will share. She dives at the small birds. The male hihi chirps angrily, flicking his ear tufts and his tail but the tui is big, has a sharp beak and is very bossy. The hihi are forced to give up.

They move down the gully, taking the occasional insect or berry as they go. At the bottom of the hill, on the edge of the old forest, they come to a sugar-water station, a caged platform with holes that are too small to let tui or korimako (bellbirds) through.

Ben has arrived already is scrubbing and washing the feeding station to ensure there is no chance of disease.

NEW ZEALAND
PASSPORT
URUWHENUA

CLASS
Aves

ORDER
Passeriformes: perching birds

FAMILY
Used to be melphagidae: honey-eaters, but is no longer certain

SCIENTIFIC NAME
Notiomystis cincta

COMMON NAME
Stitchbird

MĀORI NAME
Hihi

Ben is placing the feeder back in the feeding station. The little yellow flower on the red base of the feeder is where the hihi drink.

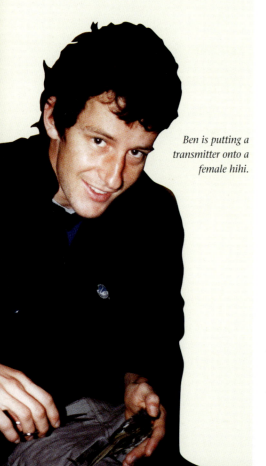

Ben is putting a transmitter onto a female hihi.

'I see you,' he says to the birds when he spots them. 'Just wait a minute.' In the middle of the platform there is a red plastic feeder dish with four yellow flowers on the side. The dish comes from the United States of America where it is used to feed hummingbirds. Ben wipes the deck of the platform, fills a bottle with a mixture of sugar and water, then tips it upside-down into the middle of the dish. A small amount flows into the sides of the dish. There are tongue-sized holes in the centre of each plastic flower. The birds have a specialised tongue that can hold quite a lot of liquid at one time. They do not need to use their beaks.

'There you go,' Ben says. 'Don't overdo it!' He picks up his things and steps back, whistling. He watches. The male bird is WARR, named after his bands — white, aluminium, red, red. There is only ever one aluminium band. It is a special one, with a unique 5-digit number for the bird on it.

The birds wait until Ben is several metres away before they hop onto the feeder. The male enters the cage first and whistles to the female. '*Stit-ch! Stit-ch!*' She joins him and they dip their bills in the sweet liquid.

The rain drips off Ben's nose. He sploshes off through the trees, humming a tune of his own.

For a long time, it was thought that hihi were in the same family as tui and korimako — the family of New Zealand honey-eaters. But that is now not certain, because even though hihi look like tui and korimako, they are genetically different. And unlike tui, korimako or any other living honey-eater in the world, hihi nest in holes in trees. This is important because it means they can only nest in mature forests where there are old trees with cavities inside them.

Sadly, that is also what makes them so vulnerable. Ship rats, especially, are ace tree-climbing, egg-and-chick burglars. From the moment the ship rats ran onto New Zealand's main islands, hihi were doomed.

When Europeans arrived in New Zealand, hihi were present only in the North Island bush and on the offshore islands. Maori valued the colourful feathers of the male and used them as decoration in cloaks. It's also said that they ate hihi — though they are so small you would need four-and-twenty for a pie!

European settlers brought the ship rat, cats and birds like pigeons which may have also carried bird diseases. It was all too much for hihi. They had no resistance. The last one was seen on the mainland in the 1880s. The only place where they remained was Hauturu, or Little Barrier Island.

Hauturu became a bird sanctuary in 1894. Like many island refuges, it is rugged. Landing there used to be difficult (it is easier now, because there is a wharf) so people and most of their pests tended to stay away. Kiore, or bush rats, were taken there by the Maori and later there were wild cats, but there were never any ship rats — and that is probably what saved hihi.

Hauturu has been made safer and safer. The last wild cats were killed in 1980 and DOC may soon remove kiore as well. Even though they are not big tree-climbers like ship rats they are still a problem. As well as hihi, Hauturu is home to many endangered creatures including weta and tuatara. When kiore are gone they will all benefit.

For now, it appears that the hihi on Hauturu are healthy. They breed in the old forests, there is plenty to eat and their numbers may be in the thousands. But what if a disease or a ship rat were to come ashore?

Since the 1980s, DOC has been trying to establish just-in-case populations in other places. First, they have a small number of hihi in a captive breeding programme at the Mount Bruce National Wildlife Centre in the Wairarapa. This helps them learn about hihi breeding behaviour and their requirements in captivity.

Second, they have moved hihi to other predator-free islands: Kapiti, Tiritiri Matangi in the Hauraki Gulf and Hen and Cuvier Islands off the east coast of Northland. For a while, DOC also had hihi on Mokoia, an island reserve in the middle of Lake Rotorua, but it was expensive to manage and disease became a problem, so the hihi were taken away.

Even with no predators, looking after hihi is not straight-forward. On Tiritiri Matangi, Cuvier and Hen, the forest is young. That means there are not many old trees with holes, so nest boxes have to be provided. In 2003, for the first time, DOC rangers on Tiritiri Matangi were pleased to find that one of the hihi nests was not in a box — a good sign. Kapiti is a little different as there are more old trees. Only two of the nests there are in boxes.

Food is an even bigger challenge. In theory, once they are in a good forest with plenty of food, hihi should be able to look after themselves, but somehow it does not seem to work like that.

The hihi top ten

The male hihi called WARR is a top Kapiti bird. He and one other are extraordinary mimics. 'They copy the other birds,' Ben says. 'They're really accurate! They tune into the sounds of the forest and imitate morepork — *screech–rrrr–*, korimako, kakariki, kaka, tui. They roll off one after another.' It's not just songs either. They copy kereru wingbeats or tui passing — *THRRRT!*

No one knows why they do this but it seems to be part of the bird's display, whether it is aggressive to other birds or showing off to females.

This female Kapiti Island hihi is called YOWIE after her leg bands — OA-YW. The male hihi below was nicknamed 'Tongue-face' because of his long tongue. It grew like that because he had something wrong with his bill.

It ain't PC, mate

It has been suggested — though no one has ever measured — that male hihi have more testosterone for their size than any other bird in the bush. When most birds mate, the male mounts the female from behind, and this happens with hihi too, but some male hihi get so amped in the breeding season that they have been seen to wrestle the female to the forest floor and mate with her face-to-face. They are the only birds known to do this.

Hihi have complex breeding arrangements, depending on circumstances. Sometimes they breed as pairs, sometimes the male has two families on the go, and sometimes they breed in groups.

Follow the leader

Fledgling hihi have a good time. They often play tag or push-and-shove. Once they are no longer fed by their parents they join a little bird crèche. Young birds need to learn what to eat and how to find it, and so some adults, mainly males, become 'teachers' and show them what to do.

Ben has watched a young fledgling copying a male. 'The male flies in so the fledgling follows; the male jumps onto a perch so the fledgling sits right next to him, touching, squeezed up as close as he can. The male starts to feed at a flower and the fledgling does exactly the same thing — it's really tight!'

Hihi are at the bottom of the pecking order, after tui and korimako, but no one is sure how much that matters. In a bad winter, if hihi do not have extra food, they die very quickly. That happened on Kapiti two years ago, when it seemed that the hihi there were doing well and the extra feeding was stopped. In a short time, there were just 11 hihi left on the island.

Greg Moorcroft, the DOC biodiversity officer on the island, believes it is a matter of numbers. Once the population gets to a good level, he says, it should be able to look after itself. Hihi breed four or five chicks in a clutch and may breed twice in a good year, so even though there is a high death rate among young birds, numbers soon go up.

On Kapiti, the birds are being fed again. 2002 was a good season, and numbers increased to around 50. Another couple of seasons may see so many hihi there that they will be able to survive even bad years without help. 'With small birds, one year makes a big difference,' Greg says. He and Ben will be watching to make sure.

A female hihi at Mount Bruce National Wildlfie Centre deals to what bugs her.

Hihi facts

- It is thought that hihi's whiskers and big eyes might be because hihi nest in holes: just like cats, they can feel where the walls are.

- Hihi are also known as stitchbirds because the 19th-century bird expert Walter Lowry Buller thought they were saying *stit-ch, stit-ch*. Hihi also make a large variety of whistles and have a warbling song.

- As they drink nectar, hihi are also pollinating flowers. When they eat berries, they also spread seed. They help keep the forest they depend on healthy and growing.

- In the wild, hihi nests are built from the bottom-up in holes in trees. They are built by the female. A nest cup rests on a base made of twigs. It can be quite an engineering feat for this little bird, who finds the twigs, drags them through the hole and fits them into place. The size of the nest depends on the size of the hole.

- The male hihi guards while she builds. Sometimes he guards several females in one area.

- The female lays three to five tiny white eggs and incubates them herself. She does most of the rearing, rushing to and fro to feed the hungry mouths with occasional help from the male. This is a dangerous time for her. She may be exhausted from all that work and more easily attacked and killed by predators. This means the chicks may die too, although sometimes if that happens, the male will take over.

A female hihi (top) and a male hihi outside the entrance to their nest hole on Hauturu.

15 The great question
The story of 42, the karearea or falcon

'You're really not going to like it,' observed Deep Thought.
  'Tell us!'
'All right,' said Deep Thought. 'The answer to the Great Question . . .'
  'Yes . . . !'
'Of Life, the Universe and Everything . . .' said Deep Thought.
  'Yes . . . !'
'Is . . .' said Deep Thought, and paused.
  'Yes . . . !'
'Is . . .'
  'Yes . . . !!! . . . ?'
'Forty-two,' said Deep Thought, with infinite majesty and calm.

— Douglas Adams
The Hitch Hiker's Guide to the Galaxy, Ch. 27

NEW ZEALAND

PASSPORT
URUWHENUA

CLASS
Aves

ORDER
Falconiformes: falcons and allies

FAMILY
Falconidae: falcons

SCIENTIFIC NAME
Falco novaeseelandiae

COMMON NAMES
New Zealand falcon, sparrowhawk, bush hawk, quail hawk

MĀORI NAME
Kārearea

42 OPENED ONE EYE. It was nearly sunrise and the last star hung over the lake. The sky was clear and cool.

She shifted from one foot to the other and fluffed her feathers. She had roosted high in a dead tree on a hillside at the end of a long valley. Below her was a road with neatly patterned farms on either side. She saw fences, patches of bush, houses and paddocks with waking sheep, cattle and deer. It was the dawn of her sixth day of freedom, Christmas Eve 2000, and she was hungry. She had taken a mouse two days ago but had had only two huhu beetles since.

She smoothed her feathers, opened her wings and was off. Flying hard, she headed towards the lake. No other New Zealand birds can match falcons for speed or their ability to twist and turn. They are ace aeronauts, masters of the airwaves, supremos of the sky!

She passed over a row of old macrocarpa trees. On the far side there was a hay paddock with large round bales like eggs on the stubble. In the corner, where a row of stalky grass had been missed by the mower, 42's sharp eyes detected a flock of small birds, goldfinches, bubbling and chattering as they hopped from seedhead to seedhead.

In an instant she made a choice. She stalled and dived, gathering speed.

The finch did not see or hear the thing that snatched him from his world. Within seconds he was gripped firmly in her talons and being carried skywards. She was headed for her roost. There, she would kill the finch, rip out his feathers and feast.

But she had made a mistake, a big one.

42 had been so busy hunting that she had not seen or heard battle

A kārearea surveys the world from a perch high in a dead tree.

Tracking kārearea

Kārearea are a protected species. It is against the law to hurt or kill them. Numbers are thought to be declining in the wild but no one is really sure.

One group, at Massey University, is using the latest technology to find out. A tiny 18-g solar-powered transmitter is attached by a harness to a bird's back and the signal is read by satellite, transmitted to France and then fed back to researchers via the internet. It's a kārearea spy network.

cries in the macrocarpas. She was trespassing on the territory of a squadron of magpies and, boy, were they *grumpy*. They were now airborne, with her in their sights.

The first blow hit her on the head. The finch dropped as she staggered in the air, utterly surprised. She was surrounded by a storm of shrieking, screaming black-and-white demons. She tried to hold her place, to rise, but was stabbed and knocked and could not gain altitude. She tumbled over and over. *Thud*. She hit the ground at speed.

'What the hell is going on?' The farmer had been having his early morning cup of tea when he heard the ruckus. He went to his doorway in time to see the magpies returning to the trees.

'Noisy bloody neighbours!' he said.

He put on his gumboots and called his dogs. They crossed the paddock. The magpies were still upset, calling and shouting.

It was the black dog that found 42. He *woofed* cautiously at her. She was a mess of speckled feathers. Her head was bleeding and she was unconscious, her beak damaged, her wings awkwardly spread. She was still breathing. 'They sure did *you* over,' the farmer said sympathetically as he nudged her with his boot. He saw the bands on her legs.

'Looks like you're one of Debbie's,' he said. 'Come on. We'll get some help.' He carefully wrapped her in his jacket and headed for the house.

42 was one of three kārearea chicks hatched in the spring of 2000 at the Wingspan Birds of Prey Trust centre in Paradise Valley, near Rotorua. Her parents were injured birds that were too damaged to go back to the wild. One of the chicks was accidentally killed by the male parent, so the other two were hand-reared for five days by Debbie Stewart, manager of the trust, and her helper, Marlia Fraser.

Once they were strong enough, the chicks were returned to the nest and fed and raised by the female parent. By 35 days old, they were full-sized and ready to fly.

They were placed in a *hack box*, a cage which they came to identify as their nest. Their food — dead sparrows and starlings — was fed through a chute so there was almost no contact with humans. All the two birds knew was each other. After a week, the front of the box was opened so they were free to hunt and fly and build up wing strength.

At first, they did not go far, but as time passed they became more confident until, one day, they did not return to the box. They were now wild birds. Until the farmer pulled up in his van Debbie and Marlia thought they had seen the last of them.

42 would have died if she had not been found. It took two months for her to mend and she will not be released again as she is now a people bird. Like her parents, she will become a breeder and her chicks will help rebuild wild populations of falcons.

42 was given her name for fun, but it is appropriate because, like '42' in *The Hitch Hiker's Guide to the Galaxy*, she has answered some big questions for her species.

One of the problems for karearea is that they kill people's parrots, pigeons, chickens and quail. Even though they could be fined $10,000 some people hate karearea so much that they shoot them.

But it's not the birds' fault. Karearea are top predators, just like cats — and people. Big invertebrates eat little invertebrates, small birds eat both, and karearea eat small birds and animals. It's a natural process and we have to find ways to make it work for people and for karearea.

That's where 42 has helped. 'She has generated an incredible amount of publicity and awareness for New Zealand falcons,' Debbie says. 'She has shown how useful karearea can be.'

Grape-eating birds cause huge losses in vineyards. Winegrowers try to stop them by using bangers, guns, scarecrows and nets. But these tactics don't always work. What they need is a self-piloting automatic bird-scarer that comes when it is called and is as obedient as a dog — a *karearea*.

In March 2001 Debbie and 42 went to Lake Chalice vineyard in Marlborough for a trial. Debbie took 42 to the vines and let her go. Up she soared, into the sky — and the grape-eaters took to the hills.

Everyone was smiling. Now the Wingspan Birds of Prey Trust will have a safe place to release karearea where there are plenty of little birds that they are *allowed* to eat. By the time the karearea are ready to fly further afield, the vines will have been harvested. Karearea may be able to be used for similar bird-scaring work at airports.

42 was a star! She appeared on TV One's *Holmes* programme and even had a wine named in her honour. It was a chardonnay called 'Flight 42' — named after the bird that chased the birds that ate the grapes that made the wine.

RANZ

The Raptor Association of New Zealand (RANZ) fosters research, rescues and restores hurt birds, and boosts and protects raptors in the wild. The Wingspan Birds of Prey Trust and the Otorohanga Kiwi House are the only places in New Zealand where karearea are bred and displayed.

Falconry

Falconry is an ancient sport where trained birds are used to kill prey for their masters. It is not permitted in New Zealand but its techniques are used by people like Debbie to assess the birds and teach fitness and hunting skills before karearea are released into the wild.

In Merrie Old England falconry was very popular and the bird you flew signalled where you stood in life. Emperors flew eagles; princes flew peregrines; yeomen flew goshawks; clergy flew sparrowhawks; ladies flew merlins and knaves flew kestrels.

Falcon facts

- Karearea are raptors, or birds of prey. In New Zealand, the most commonly seen raptor is the kahu or Australasian harrier, *Circus approximans*. Kahu also live and breed throughout Australia and the Pacific.

- New Zealand has only two endemic raptors — karearea, the New Zealand falcon or *Falco novaeseelandiae*, and ruru, the morepork, *Ninox novaeseelandiae*. Kahu and karearea are day-hunters and ruru are night birds. Ruru belong to a different order, *Strigoformes*, which includes owls.

- Falcon or harrier? Karearea or kahu? Karearea eat only freshly killed prey. They are smaller than kahu and more active fliers. The female weighs around 450 g.

  Kahu are the birds that cruise over farmland. They eat carrion as well as freshly killed prey and are often seen eating road-kill. The female weighs around 750 g.

- There are three groups of karearea. The *southern karearea* is the rarest, and is found in Fiordland, Stewart Island and the Auckland Islands. The *bush karearea* is found in the lower North Island, in Nelson and the West Coast of the South Island. The *eastern karearea* is the most numerous, and is found in eastern parts of New Zealand.

- Karearea have shorter, slightly rounded wings and longer tails than overseas falcons. They fearlessly fly after prey at high speed through bush as well as across hills and open country. Overseas falcons have been tracked by radar at speeds of up to 230 kph when diving.

- The eyesight of falcons is up to eight times more powerful than a human's. Karearea use it to catch small birds, large insects and invertebrates, lizards and rodents. They are so stroppy that they sometimes take prey six times heavier than themselves.

- Karearea are traditionally bush dwellers but they are adaptable. As long as there are safe roosts and nests, they can live on the edges of open farmland or pine plantations, especially when they have been cut over. There is more prey, more open space, good eye-spy spots and in some, such as the Kaingaroa Forest, sympathetic managers have even timetabled their programmes around the birds' breeding cycles.

- In spring, when a male karearea fancies a female, he behaves like some humans and pretends to attack her until she chases him. Instead of chocolates, he offers a freshly killed mouse to demonstrate what a good provider he will be.

- Karearea lay three or four eggs. The chicks grow quickly, changing from white to grey fluffy bundles after the first week. The female parent looks after them while the male goes out for food. When he has something, she goes to meet him and they fly together. He then drops it, she flips over to catch it and takes it to the nest. *Cool.*

- First meals are ripped up for the chicks but they are soon offered whole prey and taught to attack it savagely. They are ready to fly between 32 and 35 days, and have their full adult feathers at around 52 days. Females are ready to mate at three years. It is not known how long they live but one bird is known to have reached 17 years.

A kahu, or harrier hawk, with a killed hare.

Hunter by day, hunted by night

One of the problems for these predators, karearea, is that they are preyed upon!

Like many other creatures in this book, karearea are most easily killed at nesting time. Sometimes they nest in old dead trees but more often they set up house on the ground near a bank or on a ledge. This means that they and their chicks and eggs are then likely to be attacked by rats, stoats, ferrets, cats and possums.

Part of the problem with any bird that flies so far and nests in such inaccessible places is that it is hard to know how well they are doing or even how many there are — there may be only 400 or 500 nesting pairs of karearea but no one is sure. What they do know is that nesting sites which were once occupied are now empty, and that fewer and fewer sightings are being reported. *What is happening out there?*

This is Diamond, a two-week-old karearea chick. Diamond has the same parents as 42 and was raised in exactly the same way.

A karearea on its nest on the ground.

16 Bring on the clowns
Kea and kaka, the New Zealand parrots

The intelligent, amusing kea is the only bird we have ever set out to deliberately exterminate.

— Hal Smith,
Wild South, p. 60

'BAGS THE BOTTOM BUNK,' Jen said as she threw open the hut door.

'Have it,' Steve said. 'I'm so tired I could sleep on the floor.'

'Me too,' said Al. 'Every muscle and every bone is hurting!'

'Good to be here though,' said Jen. 'Just look at that.' She peered out the window. The last sun cast a mountain-sized shadow across the plains far below. They had climbed until they were above the bush, in the tussock and scrub zone of the Southern Alps. 'It's so *quiet* here,' she said. 'I am so looking forward to bed.'

'You'll need it,' Steve said. 'You think today was hard. Wait till tomorrow.' They looked at the mountain. Track markers climbed steeply between boulders to a high pass. Jen groaned.

Outside, five kea were sitting on rocks on the hill above the hut. They watched the trampers arrive and saw them enter the hut. There were lights and voices. *EXCELLENT.* They hopped, single file, down the hill and waited. The moon rose, flooding the landscape with a white light.

Meanwhile, the climbers had finished tea and were in their bunks in sleeping bags. Jen was reading with a torch. Steve was already snoring and Al was drifting off. Jen switched off the torch and closed her eyes.

The moment the light went off, the waiting kea were onto the steeply pitched corrugated iron roof.

'WHEEE!' They slid down with loud screams, flapped their way back to the ridge and *'WHEEE!'* — down they went again. They shrieked and yelled and thudded. *'KEE-AAA!'*

Inside the hut, three trampers stared at the darkness.

'Nooo,' Steve moaned. 'Kea.'

'Just wait,' Al said. 'They'll get sick of it — they'll soon go away.'

'YEE-Har!' The noise continued.

Then it stopped.

'Thank God,' Jen said, and closed her eyes again.

'BOOM!' A stone hit the roof and bounced down and off the edge. The kea had decided to go bowling. *'RATTLE! TUNK-A-TUNK-A.'* The mirth was deafening. There was more sliding and shrieking. The kea were having a ball.

Kea clashes

Kea *do* cause problems. They wreck rubbish bins and scatter the contents, they tear wipers and rubber seals off cars, let tyres down and shred motorcycle seats. They show what happens when wild animals and people live close to each other.

In the wild, kea are mainly vegetarians that eat grubs and insects on the side. But they are not fussy. They eat anything they can find — trampers' lunches, food left in tramping huts or rubbish from a bin.

And that's where the trouble starts. Human food is like junk food for kea and they get more energy than they need in a very short time. They don't have to look for anything else — and then they get bored. Young males, especially, have nothing to do. They become hoons and vandals and the law — DOC — has to step in. Taking the ringleader away often solves the problem — for a while, at least.

- Wild kea should not be fed — ever!
- Rubbish and kea should be kept apart.
- Don't leave your car in the bush when kea are about.
- Kea are incredibly bright and especially love yellow bendy things. If it looks like a toy, a kea will want to play with it. Look out! Kea about!

'Can't stand it,' said Jen. 'I've got to get some sleep.'

She switched on her torch, jumped off the bunk in her sleeping bag and waddled to the other side of the hut. She grabbed the broom.

'SHUT UP!' she yelled, thumping it on the corrugated iron.

There was a stunned silence.

'That's done it,' Steve said. 'Good on you, Jen.'

'Hey, look!' Al said.

A kea was hanging upside-down from the top of the window looking into the room. The trampers looked at the kea, and the kea looked at the trampers. Then, as if a signal had been given, the first stone began to rattle down the roof again. *'KEE-HAR!'*

Kea and kaka are both parrots and belong to the *nestorinae* family. They are largely daytime birds but will also venture out at night in fine weather and a full moon.

Both are listed as threatened species.

Kea, *Nestor notabilis*, are alpine parrots, birds of the South Island high country. They are inquisitive and sociable and among the most intelligent birds in the world. They like to know what's going on and, if possible, take things apart. They have very strong beaks.

That combination has brought them a lot of grief. They are the only bird we have *deliberately* tried to wipe out altogether.

In the late 1800s they were blamed for killing sheep and the birds were described as maniacal, bloodthirsty, evil murderers. The government authorised local councils to pay a bounty of between 2/6 and £1 per beak. Shepherds and musterers carried firearms and some became full-time bounty-hunters. By the time common sense asserted itself, 29,000 birds had been slaughtered and there was no need to carry guns any more — there were few kea to be seen.

There are at least 5000 kea in the wild. They can be found all the way from Fiordland to northern Marlborough, but because they live in such mountainous places it has been very hard for anyone to count them. Kea became fully protected in 1986. They live for around 15 years.

Kaka are the kea's smaller forest-dwelling cousins — kea weigh about 900 g and kaka about 500 g. Kaka were valued by Maori as a food and for their beautiful feathers but were still common when Europeans came to New Zealand. By 1930, once the bush had been felled and the predators had moved in, they were confined to just a few areas.

There are two subspecies, the North Island kaka, *Nestor meridionalis septentrionalis*, and the South Island kaka, *Nestor meridionalis meridionalis*. Both are brown-green with flashes of orange and scarlet under the wings. They are strong fliers that hop, rather than walk, when they are on the ground. The South Island bird is more brightly coloured, a little larger and still relatively common in forests south of Nelson. North Island kaka are found in large mainland forests such as Pureora and Whirinaki but are mainly on offshore islands, especially Little Barrier, Great Barrier and Kapiti.

Kaka nest in holes in trees and need large mature forests, both for their nests and for feeding. They prefer lower and mid-altitude bush and use their powerful beaks to rip open rotting logs to get at insects and larvae. Like most parrots, they use their feet to hold food to their beaks. They also eat seeds and fruit, and have a brush-tipped tongue which allows them to harvest nectar. As they feed, they are pollinating the forest — it needs them for its health as much as they need it.

Like kea, kaka are totally protected.

A kaka feeding on a southern rata.

Lake Rotoiti mainland island

825 hectares alongside Lake Rotoiti in Nelson Lakes National Park are being managed to keep numbers of stoats, rats, possums and wasps down. The benefit to kaka has been immediate, with a dramatic increase in nesting success compared with kaka outside the managed area. Wasps affect kaka because they eat the honeydew, a sweet syrup which is found on beech trees that kaka also eat.

Kaka at play

Kaka are playful and aerobatic. They do bird bungy-jumps. They hang upside-down from a branch with their wings spread and let go. They fall, do a somersault and return to the branch before hitting the ground. *WHEE!*

They are also noisy, especially early and late in the day when they feed in flocks. They have a range of musical calls, whistles, chortles and *squarrks*.

Parrots and disease

All of New Zealand's parrots, including the small kakariki and the kakapo, could be killed very quickly by diseases imported with pet parrots. In 2002 the psittacine pox virus was found among rosellas and birds on three Auckland properties and they had to be destroyed by Ministry of Agriculture and Fisheries staff to prevent its spread. The danger is greatest when birds or their eggs are smuggled into the country.

17 A long slow start
A tale of a tuatara

IT'S A LAZY DAY on North Brother Island in Cook Strait. A sea breeze ruffles the trees and ripples the waters. A young female tuatara lies in the part-sun, part-shade outside her burrow. She does not know it, but deep inside, a cell is dividing in a new, different way. An egg forms, and then another and another, until there are 12 altogether. She is becoming a teenager.

For three years, the eggs grow. And all that time, the tuatara goes about her life, resting by day and hunting at night. In summer she shares a burrow with a small seabird, a fairy prion. They keep similar hours and mostly ignore each other but the tuatara does well out of the deal because the prion's droppings attract insects and she likes to eat insects. In fact, she likes to eat most things — insects, lizards, weta, frogs, prion eggs, baby prion and even baby tuatara! She's not picky.

While the eggs grow, so does she. She becomes longer and heavier. Once a year she sheds her skin at the back, then grows a little more. She will not reach full size until she is 30.

But just now she is nearly 16 and the eggs are ready. They are big and yolky and contain food for the baby tuatara that will grow inside them. It is summer and the nights are warm. She becomes restless. It is time to seek a mate.

He is not far away, beside a heap of rocks, guarding the entrance to his burrow. His body is swelled and his crest filled out. He is a handsome beast, olive-yellow with small bright yellow spots on his skin. He walks around her, his legs stiff.

A male tuatara does not have a penis. He mates by lying on top of the female pressing the opening under his tail (called a *vent* or *cloaca*) hard against hers while he transfers sperm into her body. After a while she wriggles away and wanders off, back to her patch and the fairy prion.

In the next weeks, the eggs move out of her ovary and into her oviduct, where they meet up with the sperm. Each egg is fertilised by a sperm, and that is the beginning of a new tuatara.

But tuatara didn't get where they are today by hurrying . . .

It will be almost two years before these little fellows see the light of day — or night. For ten months, while a soft, papery shell forms around each egg, the female tuatara carries them inside her body.

Winter passes. The fairy prion has gone. It is cold and the tuatara spends a lot of time keeping very still, often in the burrow and, when the sun peeps through, outside on the rocks.

In spring, when the earth is soft and beginning to warm up, she feels restless again.

NEW ZEALAND
PASSPORT
URUWHENUA

CLASS
Reptilia

ORDER
Sphenodontia

FAMILY
Sphenodontidae

SCIENTIFIC NAMES (TWO SPECIES)
Sphenodon punctatus
Sphenodon guntheri

MĀORI NAMES
Tuatara, tuatete, ngārara

A tuatara nest at the Southland Museum tuatarium.

A young tuatara corkscrews into the light.

One night she begins to make a nest in a sheltered spot beside some logs. She scrapes like a dog, spraying dirt behind her as she digs a hole 150 mm deep. She lays the eggs in the nest. They are 20–30 mm long and creamy white, though they will soon become brown and stained.

She fills the hole with grass and soil and returns every night for a few days to fuss and guard it in case another female tuatara should accidentally dig it up and smash the eggs.

Then she forgets all about it. Already, her body is making the eggs which will be laid four years from now.

Summer comes.

Then autumn.

And winter.

The eggs are safe in the ground and all the while, inside each shell, a tiny tuatara is taking shape and growing. When it is cold, growth slows right down, but then summer returns and the days and nights are hot. It is 11 months since the eggs were laid.

For about a month, the eggs have been swelling with moisture from the soil. Each egg is now as tight as a drum. A small spike called a *caruncle* has appeared on the first little tuatara's nose. Something is about to happen!

At last he is ready. He uses his spike like a drill, to make a hole in the shell. He is out. But — hey! He is the first of the 12 to hatch and he is alone in the dark, deep in the ground. He wriggles and squirms and corkscrews upwards to the surface.

For the first time, his large round eyes see the sky. He is a wrinkly, speckled, beak-headed, wedge-toothed miniature tuatara. He is 100 mm long and weighs only 5 grams. In the middle of his head he has a primitive silver-white third eye which will be covered over with scales as he grows. His caruncle will fall off in two weeks. Until he grows bigger, he will lie low at night and be active by day to avoid being eaten by adult tuatara. If all goes well for him, he will live to be 100, maybe more.

For now, there is no time to lose. Tuatara are not known for their speed, but it's very dangerous here and he could be eaten on his first day out. He heads for the nearest logs. He is on his own. But he knows what to do.

Events just like this have been happening in the land mass we call New Zealand for about 225 million years. Like so many New Zealand animals, tuatara are absolutely, amazingly, astonishingly unique! Their ancestors, which looked much the same as this tuatara and his mum, shared the Earth with dinosaurs — and were the only ones of their family that did not die out when the age of reptiles ended 65 million years ago.

Tuatara are not lizards. In 1831, British taxonomists thought they were, but by 1867 Dr Albert Günther of the British Museum realised that they are the only living members of what was once the largest reptile family, *Sphenodontia*. Tuatara are relicts from Gondwana and probably first came overland to New Zealand from South America as long ago as 180 million years, when this country was still joined to Antarctica. When the dinosaurs and reptiles disappeared, the tuatara in mammal-free New Zealand were the only ones left.

Until humans arrived, that is. Once the Polynesian rat, kiore, put foot on the mainland, tuatara were in trouble. Kiore do not often eat adult tuatara but they gobble up eggs and hatchlings. By the time Europeans arrived, tuatara were found mostly only on island fortresses ringed by vertical cliffs and washed by rough seas.

There are two species of tuatara, *Sphenodon punctatus* (which means 'spotted') which are larger and are greyish-green, and *Sphenodon guntheri* which are smaller and olive-grey. *Sphenodon* means 'wedge-tooth', referring to the tuatara's chisel-like teeth.

Sphenodon guntheri are very rare. Until the late 1980s there were only 350, on four-hectare North Brother Island in Cook Strait. In 1989, Victoria University of Wellington started a captive incubation programme using eggs of both species from the wild. They hatch young tuatara and raise them to five years old before they let them go. This gives them a head start. In 1995, 68 were transferred to a secret island in the Marlborough Sounds to start a second population.

In 1998 a third population of *S. guntheri* was started when 55 adults and juveniles were released on the 25-hectare island of Matiu (Somes) in Wellington Harbour. It was a HUGE day. Hundreds of people came, including people from the Wellington Tenths Trust who are descended from Te Atiawa Maori who once lived on Matiu. They were proud to welcome the tuatara back.

Tuatara teeth!

It is said that you can tell tuatara scientists by their scarred and bandaged fingers! Tuatara have powerful jaws and awesome teeth. Once they clamp shut on your hand, they don't let go in a hurry. They have two rows of teeth in the top and one row in the bottom. When they close up, the bottom teeth slide into the gap between the top ones. *Ouch ouch OUCH!*

To make it worse, the seabirds that share tuatara tunnels also bite, and so do stinging centipedes! *Ouch* again! Some scientists now use tennis balls on sticks when they have to get tuatara from burrows.

During their lives, tuatara teeth are gradually worn down and are not replaced. Old tuatara end up toothless!

Matiu is a good place with heaps of tuatara food — lots of skinks and tree weta. Artificial tunnels had been made but in no time at all the tuatara spread across the island, making their own burrows in all sorts of places, including under buildings, garages and walls.

Richard Anderson is a DOC ranger on the island. He knows some of the tuatara very well.

'One of the males,' he says, 'has set up camp in a burrow under the concrete floor of a garage. There's a downpipe there and every time it rains, he sits under that downpipe and lets the water hose over him. He's a hard case. He actually puts his head right up the pipe!'

The tuatara seem content but DOC will know they are truly secure the day the first tuatara babies are seen. Richard expects that to be very soon. 'There's a box of chocolate fish in the freezer for the first person who spots one!' he says. They are probably there already, hiding just like little tuatara on his island.

Left: Lorna Kanavakoa and her whanau holding a box of tuatara on the wharf on Matiu.
Below: Koro Tamarapa leads some of the party onto Matiu. The tuatara are in the cardboard box.

Tuatara facts

- There are about 100,000 tuatara left in the world. That may seem a lot but there used to be *millions*. The largest population is on Stephens Island in Cook Strait, at the top of the South Island (see 'The rock group', Chapter 6). The island's open grassy paddocks used to be for sheep and are now ideal for nesting tuatara because they are warm. It is thought there are up to 50,000 *Sphenodon punctatus* there.

- Tuatara grow until they are about 30 years old. They live anywhere from 70 to 100 years and possibly much longer.

  How will we know? In the past, tuatara have been identified by toe-marking, much the same as frogs. Recently, small cylindrical chips called PIT tags have been used. They are inserted beneath the skin and have a unique electronic barcode which can be read by waving a scanner over the tuatara. Just like going through the checkout at the supermarket!

- Males are bigger than females, and can be up to 610 mm from beak to tail-tip and weigh up to 1.2 kg. Females are only half that, with narrower heads.

A Stephens Island tuatara.

- 'Tuatara' is a Maori word meaning 'spiny back'. The spines look prickly but are actually soft and bendy. They are more obvious on the males, and stand up during courtship and when the tuatara is feeling aggressive or defensive. Pre-European Maori were in awe of tuatara and believed they possessed supernatural powers.

- Tuatara are cool! It's said they are 'cold-blooded' but actually they are *poikilothermic*, which means their temperature follows that of the air around them. When it's cold in winter, they slow right down although they don't hibernate. They can go six months without feeding and have been seen to breathe only once in an hour. They don't like to get too hot, and have a heart-rate of nine to 10 beats per minute. *Slooow.*

  In fact, tuatara are way cooler than most reptiles, which function best between 25° and 38°C. Tuatara do well at between 12° and 17°C.

- Temperature even affects the sex of tuatara eggs! When they are incubated in a laboratory at 21°C, almost 100 percent of them are female, but if the temperature is raised to 22°C, 100 percent are male.

A tuatara checkup on Whatapuke Island in the Poor Knights Islands by Ian McFadden.

- The tuatara has a third eye in the middle of its head although in adults it is covered up. It does not see but is more like a sensor of light and dark. It may help regulate temperature by telling tuatara when it's had too much sun.

- If an enemy grabs a tuatara's tail, the tail breaks off and wriggles around. While the enemy is distracted the tuatara gets away. In time, a new, different tail grows. Male tuatara sometimes pull each other's tails off, and they also scratch and bite each other. They are often battered and battle-scarred.

- Tuatara were the first non-bird native species to be protected by law, in 1895. It is illegal to handle them or remove them from the places where they are found. Unfortunately, overseas reptile collectors will pay a lot of money for tuatara so DOC, the New Zealand Police and New Zealand Customs are always on the lookout for smugglers, who are jailed and fined when convicted.

Matiu (Somes)

The two names of the island reflect the two peoples of New Zealand. The name 'Matiu' is said to have been given by the Maori explorer Kupe, a long, long time ago, in honour of his daughter. 'Somes' was given in 1839 after Mr Joseph Somes of the New Zealand Company, which brought many Pakeha to New Zealand.

Matiu/Somes has been a Maori settlement, an animal quarantine station, a human quarantine station, a prison camp in World War I and a military base in World War II. It is now an open scientific reserve managed by DOC — and home to special tuatara.

Below: This is Matiu.

Above right: Tuatara habitat on Kawhitu (Stanley Island) in the Mercury Islands group. Rabbits have eaten a lot of the undergrowth.

The great gecko

Tuatara are not lizards although they have a lot in common with them. Tuatara have been around so long, they are related to the *ancestors* of modern lizards. New Zealand has two lizard families, the geckos and the skinks.

New Zealand's largest gecko is probably extinct. It is called kawekaweau or *Hoplodactylus delcourti*. There were two reports of it in the early 1800s, but after that, nothing — no sightings and only two mysterious, tiny fossil bones. People began to think it was a myth.

Then, in 1979, a man named Alain Delcourt found a huge stuffed gecko in a museum in France. No one knew anything about it. In the end it was identified as a species of *Hoplodactylus*, a genus known only in New Zealand — it was the missing giant gecko!

Maori were rightly in awe of it. Kawekaweau was as large as a cat and would have been a serious killer of animals and birds, with a very large bite! The stuffed specimen shows us that it was beautifully striped, brown and red. At least one herpetologist still searches for it now and then. Like the takahe, it might be out there somewhere!

Duvaucel's gecko and a grand skink.

Geckos and skinks

New Zealand has 16 species of gecko (family *Gekkonidae*) and 28 species of skinks (family *Scincidae*).

Geckos have chunky bodies, broad heads, baggy granular skins which they periodically moult, wide toes for climbing, and large unblinking eyes.

Skinks have streamlined, polished-looking bodies, pointed heads, fish-like scales which are replaced one at a time, thin toes for running, and small, blinkable eyes.

Both geckos and skinks live in a wide range of habitats from tree and mountain tops to stony banks. They are often beautifully coloured and patterned.

Like tuatara, geckos may have been in New Zealand more than 85 million years. Skinks may have been here 40 million years.

Geckos' complicated feet enable them to climb walls, ceilings and even up glass. They make a range of sounds, from faint chirps to loud barks. If you hear screams coming from your living room one night, it might not be a TV thriller but the yells of an angry gecko cornered by your cat! *Quick! Save it!*

The giant kawekaweau on display. A live green gecko is underneath.

18 All at sea
The albatross of Taiaroa Head

At length did cross an albatross
Thorough the fog it came
As if it had been a Christian soul
We hailed it in God's name.

It ate the food it ne'er had eat,
And round and round it flew.
The ice did split with a thunder-fit;
The helmsman steered us through!

And a good south wind sprung up behind;
The albatross did follow
And every day, for food or play
Came to the mariners' hollo!

— Samuel Taylor Coleridge,
'The Rime of the Ancient Mariner', 1797

Taiaroa Head, September 1988

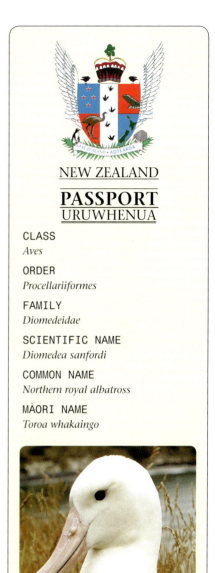

NEW ZEALAND

PASSPORT
URUWHENUA

CLASS
Aves

ORDER
Procellariiformes

FAMILY
Diomedeidae

SCIENTIFIC NAME
Diomedea sanfordi

COMMON NAME
Northern royal albatross

MĀORI NAME
Toroa whakaingo

THE WIND LICKS HIS LEGS and tugs his wings. It is an invitation. *Come.* All of his short life he has been preparing for this moment, and any minute now Buttons, a young northern royal albatross, or toroa, will leap into space from the top of a cliff.

His mother, 60-year-old Grandma, is the oldest known wild bird in the world. In mid-November the year before, she laid one slightly pitted, faintly red-speckled round egg in the middle of a soil and grass nest on the edge of the exposed and windy Taiaroa Head near Dunedin, on the east coast of the South Island.

For almost three months the chick grew inside the pale white globe of the egg while Grandma and her mate took turns to warm it with their soft underbellies, until at last he was ready.

It took seven hard days of squeaking and pecking before the shell parted and fell away to reveal his wet, naked-chick beauty. He dried in the warm January wind, a tiny, comical fluff-covered cone with a black hooked beak and a crooked black smile.

He was named Buttons because he was small. He was very hungry. For five weeks Grandma and her mate worked wall-to-wall shifts, one at sea feeding and getting him food, the other guarding him at the nest.

After that, he was left alone for longer and longer periods. His parents brought him oily meals of chopped-up squid and fish which they regurgitated into his bill. He grew larger, until he was heavier

than either of them. His baby-soft down became sleek flying feathers and his stumpy chick's limbs lengthened into narrow, elegant wings. He had become a young bird.

Like a human teenager, he began to rev up. From about six months old, he started to flex his muscles, to stand and stretch on the nest, waving his wings against the wind's resistance. He experimented with small vertical hops, and gradually bounced higher and higher as his wings strengthened. Sometimes he was a metre off the ground.

Towards the end of eight months, his parents started to feed him less and the excess weight fell away, and then one week, without warning or farewell, they did not come back. Buttons waited several days and cried a bit from hunger and frustration, but the only ones to hear were equally abandoned young birds and a small group of people looking down from the observation platform above.

'He'll be right,' one said. 'He's nearly ready.'

He was on his own.

And so, after nine months, Buttons waddles to the cliff edge. He looks over and stands a while, bobbing like a learner diver on the end of the high board, his wings spread.

Far below the harbour lies in the sun. It is blue-green, deep, and rich with food. Suddenly, without ceremony, he crouches, does a small jump, tilts forward and falls . . . The updraught catches him, cupping his body and holding him up. He wobbles. Then, magically, his wings adjust and trim and balance. His feet float like rudders. He soars and begins to lift and glide. He could not return if he wanted. He is on his way to the landless blue line where the sky meets the sea.

There is a cheer from the platform. 'Good luck!' someone calls. 'Fly well! Come back!'

Getoutahere!

The food albatross chicks receive from their parents is a mix of oil, squid and fish. It's sticky and it pongs. When a chick is disturbed or anxious it throws up all over the visitor. *Phoo.*

A partly-fledged seven-month-old toroa chick flexes its wings. On the right, a juvenile toroa practises for the big day, just like Buttons.

an undignified splash in the briny. When an attempt fails, a rescue boat is sent out and the bedraggled would-be glider is returned to the cliff to sulk and rest. A couple of days later, it tries again and sooner or later it's off.

Buttons spent the next six years at sea. In that time, he travelled an estimated 1,140,000 kilometres using wind-and-wing power and did not once set foot on land. He went east, to the South Atlantic, for his first winter and then on, around the earth with the west wind. He learned to eat, drink and sleep on the ocean. He steered by the sun and the stars and somehow, deep inside, not only remembered when to return to Taiaroa Head, but also how to get there.

His homecoming was not graceful. He returned in 1994 with a three-point landing on his beak. Some birds, their legs weak after long periods at sea, do worse and cartwheel to a halt. It must feel strange after all that air and water, to land on something solid, but they don't break anything.

For the next few years, Buttons returned every summer for a couple of months to spend time with other young birds — not jamming but *gamming* — which is just another way of saying 'hanging out'. When he was 12, later than most, he mated and the cycle began again. Toroa mate for life, so maybe he was just making sure of his choice.

Accidents aside, Buttons and his mate may breed for another 25 or more years and, if he takes after his mother, maybe longer. He never saw Grandma again because her clock finally ran down. She left the headland in June 1989 and did not come back. She had been banded in 1937 at the estimated age of ten. Buttons was her last chick.

Shirley Webb with Grandma and her two-week-old chick Buttons, Taiaroa Head, Autumn 1989.

Buttons, 2003

Buttons did not raise a chick in 2003. His mate laid an egg and while he was having his turn on the nest, she went to sea. Where did she go? *Did she forget the time?* Eighteen days passed and DOC staff despaired. She should have been back in 10 days, max. Something had happened for sure. They swapped her egg with a dummy because they knew one bird could not raise a chick on its own. They put the good egg under a female named the Chile Bird.

As a youngster on her first flight, the Chile Bird was found by a fisherman far out at sea. She was distressed and he took her to Chile, where schoolchildren looked after her until she could fly again. Although she returned to health, she has never laid an egg. That doesn't stop her being a good parent, so she and her mate were given Buttons' chick to bring up.

Two days after the eggs were swapped, Buttons' mate returned. *Too late.*

Toroa breed one year and rest the next, but if they fail to rear a chick they have another go the following year. That is why Buttons and his mate would be expected back in 2004.

That is also why there was a record number of birds in the Taiaroa Head colony in 2003 — at the end of February there were 105 albatross present, counting adolescents, non-breeders and 27 newly-hatched chicks. This was because a number of chicks died in 2002, reasons unknown. The unsuccessful adult toroa tried again, joining those who would have bred in 2003 anyway.

Superstitions and paper clips

It was once thought that albatross were the souls of dead sailors wandering the oceans, so killing one was very bad luck. The ancient mariner in the poem at the beginning of this chapter brought a curse upon himself and his companions when he shot an arrow into the albatross that followed their ship. Like a lost soul, he was made to wander the Earth telling and retelling his story.

However, sealers, whalers and bird hunters in the Southern Hemisphere in the late 1700s and 1800s were not at all superstitious. They killed albatross to provide specimens for museums and collectors, as well as for body parts — skins were made into feather rugs, feet could be used as tobacco pouches, hollow wing-bones made pipe stems, breast feathers made warm muffs, and beaks were made into paper clips!

Maori also killed albatross. The bones were used to fashion spear tips, nose flutes and toggles, and the feathers were highly valued adornments.

The Taiaroa toroa

There are two species of royal albatross, the northern, *Diomedea sanfordi*, and the southern, *Diomedea epomophora* and they and their cousins, the wandering albatross, share the Maori name *toroa*. This can be confusing so this story mostly uses their English names.

Toroa are sometimes referred to as 'great albatross' because they are the largest seabirds in the world. They have wingspans of up to 3.3 m, can weigh as much as 8 kg, and have been clocked at speeds of up to 115 kph. Scientists using satellite telemetry to follow them are astonished at the distances they cover in one day and have tracked them right around the planet.

The northern royal albatross is a little smaller and has more black on its back than the southern. There are between 6500 and 7000 northern royal albatross breeding pairs, mainly in the Chathams. They also make up the main population at Taiaroa Head.

The southern royal albatross breed mainly on Campbell Island. There are between 6300 and 7800 breeding pairs.

Taiaroa Head is the only place in the world where albatross breed on the mainland. The first albatross was seen there in 1914, but the first egg was not laid until 1920. It disappeared, and for 16 years every time eggs were laid they were eaten or broken by humans or animals. When at last a chick hatched, in 1935, it was killed by a dog.

After that, Dr Lance Richdale, the man who studied hoiho, camped with the birds at breeding time. He was rewarded by the sight of the first young albatross take-off in 1938. The colony became a reserve in 1953 and is now managed by DOC. It is fenced and trapped to keep rats, cats and stoats away from eggs and chicks. Eleven bird species breed in the area and fur seals can be seen on the beach below.

A pair of adult northern royal albatross at Taiaroa Head.

Albatross facts

- New Zealand has more seabird life than any other country in the world. Being land-lubbers, most people don't see a lot of it except when the birds come onshore to breed, and because many nest on offshore islands, often not even then.

- Just under half the 85 seabird species that breed on New Zealand islands are endemic — they nest nowhere else in the world. That includes 14 species of albatross and 35 petrels and shearwaters, as well as penguins, gannets, shags, gulls and terns. Of course, the birds are *citizens of the world*. They don't recognise human boundaries or laws.

- For a seabird, being at sea is more normal than being on land. Albatross will spend over 85 percent of their lives offshore, and if it were not for the need to nest, they would probably just stay there. Their preferred zone is the Southern Ocean because it is rich in currents that carry their favourite food — squid, octopus, salps and fish.

- Albatross seem to have an in-built map for the best food at any time of year. They also have keen eyes and sharp noses — they soon detect fishing boats that are tossing out fish scraps and detour to pick up fast fish snacks.

- There are 24 internationally recognised species of albatross. Sadly, their fondness for an easy meal is driving many of them to extinction. For any seabird, there are constant hazards such as pollution from oil, pesticides and rubbish — but for albatross and petrels the greatest danger is that they will die accidental and unnecessary deaths behind a fishing boat.

- Albatross belong to the order Procellariiformes, or tubenoses. 'Tubenose' refers to the way salt is removed from their bodies — there is no fresh water in the middle of the ocean. The salt runs down tubes inside the bill and drips off the end. *Do, dey habn't god colds.*

- Albatross like to hang out when they are on land. Teenage albatross stand in circles and appear to chat; during courting and greeting rituals, some species stand face-to-face, spread their wings and seem to dance; some tilt their heads back and bray like donkeys; others clack and clapper their bills. They are *not* quiet neighbours.

- They don't know it, but sometimes in the southern oceans, albatross are in the company of distant cousins, the penguins. They once had a common ancestor, but over 65 million years ago the albatross went skyward to become king of the air, while the penguin dived deep to become lord of the sea.

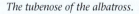

The tubenose of the albatross.

Death at sea

It is estimated that tens of thousands of albatross and petrel die each year in the Southern Ocean. Long-lining fishing boats set thousands of baited hooks at one time. The birds dive for them, become hooked and drown. Others are killed when they are snagged on wire ropes behind trawlers. Pirates fishing illegally for toothfish are especially a problem because they work without care for what they are doing.

Albatross and petrels do not breed quickly enough to replace the birds killed in this way. Some species could become extinct if no action is taken. A lot of these deaths can be prevented simply by changing fishing methods.

Some fishing companies are using bird-scaring banners called *tori lines* behind the boats. They also put the lines out at night and weight the lines so they sink too rapidly for the birds to take the bait. Albatross will feed on any night except the very darkest, so the boats need to keep lights off and avoid the full moon as well.

The last word

This is what Samuel Taylor Coleridge said in 1797:

*Farewell, farewell! but this I tell
To thee, thou Wedding Guest!
He prayeth well, who loveth well
Both man and bird and beast.*

*He prayeth best, who loveth best
All things both great and small;
For the dear God who loveth us,
He made and loveth all.*

Find out more

- Go to your library. It's an excellent place to start. Some of the books used to help write this book are listed over the page. There are many others.

- Use the internet. It gets better and better. You can either do a search using a search engine (such as www.searchnz.co.nz) or visit some of the following:

  www.kcc.org.nz
  :   This is the Forest and Bird Kiwi Conservation Club site. It not only has heaps of information, it also has excellent references.

  www.learnz.org.nz
  :   Go on virtual field trips with the team at Learnz.

  www.doc.govt.nz
  :   This is a huge site. It's also excellent with good links.

  www.mtbruce.doc.govt.nz
  :   This is another good DOC site.

  www.biodiversity.govt.nz
  :   This is also a government site with lots of information.

  www.forest-bird.org.nz and www.nzgeographic.co.nz
  :   Use these to find out what's in the excellent *Forest and Bird* and *New Zealand Geographic* magazines.

  www.nzbirds.com
  :   This is good for background information.

  www.converge.org.nz/hoiho and www.penguin.net.nz
  :   The first is the site of the Yellow-Eyed Penguin Trust.

  www.kakaporecovery.org.nz and www.parrot.co.nz
  :   Go to these sites to find out about kakapo and other parrots.

  www.wingspan@xtra.co.nz
  :   This stylish site can tell you all about karearea and other birds of prey.

  www.kiwirecovery.org.nz
  :   Find out lots of information about kiwi.

  www.tiritirimatangi.org.nz
  :   Find out about takahe and the other amazing animals on Tiritiri Matangi.

- Talk to local experts.

- Magazines such as *Forest and Bird* and *New Zealand Geographic* are great for all sorts of information and excellent pictures.

- Newspapers, especially on-line ones, are great for up-to-date news. The *New Zealand Herald* has an excellent on-line archive at www.nzherald.co.nz (go to 'search') and others like the *Wairarapa Times-Age* at http://times-age.co.nz are very good as well.

Useful books

In addition to sources listed on the previous page, the following were frequently consulted in gathering material for *A Bird in the Hand*.

Bellamy, David and Springett, Peter with Hayden, Peter. *Moa's Ark, the Voyage of New Zealand*. Viking, 1990

Checklist of the birds of New Zealand and the Ross Dependancy, Antarctica. Random Century New Zealand Ltd, 1990

Gaze, Peter. *Rare and Endangered New Zealand Birds*. Canterbury University Press, 1974

Gill, Brian and Martinson, Paul. *New Zealand's Extinct Birds*. Random Century, 1991

Gill, Brian and Whitaker, Tony. *New Zealand Frogs and Reptiles*. David Bateman, 1996

Gill, Brian and Moon, Geoff. *New Zealand's Unique Birds*. Reed Books, 1999

McCulloch, Beverley and Cox, Geoffrey J. *Moas: Lost Giants of New Zealand*. HarperCollins, 1992

Morris, Rod and Smith, Hal. *Wild South: Saving New Zealand's Endangered Birds*. TVNZ in association with Century Hutchinson NZ Ltd, 1988

Spencer Davis, Lloyd. *The Plight of the Penguin*. Longacre Press, 2001.

Illustration credits

Key: t = top; m = middle (l–r); c = centre (t–b); b = bottom; l = left; r = right; DOC = Department of Conservation *Te Papa Atawhai*; Hocken = Hocken Library, *Uare Taoka o Hakena*, University of Otago, Dunedin.

Most illustrations are courtesy of the Department of Conservation *Te Papa Atawhai*. These acknowledge both the department and the photographer, where known. Some illustrations have been clearcut from larger photographs: in these instances the original photographer is acknowledged. Small drawings and silhouettes are by the author.

5: Hocken c/n E4517/22; 6 from t: D. Mudge/DOC, DOC, D. Merton/DOC, DOC; 7tr: R. Morris/DOC; 7br: J. Hunt; 8t: J. Hunt, 8br: B. Ahern/DOC; 9–11: J. Hunt; 12: DOC; 14: D. Merton/DOC; 15: D. Merton/DOC; 16: D. Merton/DOC; 17: D. Merton/DOC; 18: D. Merton/DOC; 19: R. Morris/DOC, 19t: C. Smuts-Kennedy/DOC; 20: Hocken c/n B586; 21t: D. Merton/DOC, 21tr: D. Merton/DOC, 21br: A.K. Munn/DOC; 22–23: D. Merton/DOC; 24: R. Morris/DOC; 25: D. Veitch/DOC; 26t: M. Bayliss/DOC, 26br: S. Heppelthwaite/DOC; 27: D.P. Murray/DOC; 28–29: M. Bayliss/DOC; 30: R. Morris/DOC; 31tl: D. Merton/DOC, 31tr: J. Hunt, 31bl: R. Morris/DOC, 31br: M. Bayliss/DOC; 32tl: A. Reith/DOC, 32bl: M.J. Williams/DOC, 32rc: A. Reith/DOC, 32rb: A. Reith/DOC; 33: M.J. Williams/DOC; 34: D. Gleeson/DOC; 35-36: C.R. Veitch/DOC; 37: R. Morris/DOC; 38t: J. O'Brien/DOC, 38br: F. Bruemmer/DOC; 39: R. Morris/DOC; 40: P.J. Moore/DOC; 41: J. Darby/DOC; 42tr: Hocken c/n S03/071c, 42br: J. O'Brien/DOC; 43tl: R. Morris/DOC, 43tm: C.A. Fleming/DOC, 43tr: R. Morris/DOC, 43br: N. Peat/DOC; 44: I.G. Crook/DOC; 45: R. Parrish/DOC; 46: DOC; 47: J.L. Kendrick/DOC; 48t: DOC, 48b: R. Parrish/DOC; 49t: J.L. Kendrick/DOC, 49b: J. Hunt; 50–53: S. King/DOC; 54: I. Flux/DOC; 55tr: S. Cranwell, 55bl: S. King/DOC, 55br: C. Ward/DOC; 56: DOC; 57bl: D. Veitch/DOC, 57br: S. King/DOC; 58: J. Clarkson/DOC; 59: P. Topping; 60t: J. Hunt, 60bl: J. Clarkson/DOC, 60br: J. Clarkson/DOC; 61: J. Clarkson/DOC; 62–63: B. Lloyd; 64l: S. Baker/Waikato Times, 64br: N. Patrick/DOC; 65–66: B. Lloyd; 67tl: D. Veitch/DOC, 67tr: C. Smuts-Kennedy/DOC, 67bl: J.L. Kendrick/DOC, 67br: DOC; 68: M. Jones/Roving Tortoise Photos; 69: R. Morris/DOC; 70t: J. Hunt, 70br: DOC; 71tr: J.N. Jolly/DOC, 71br: T. Bliss/DOC; 72tl: C.D. Roderick/DOC, 72tm: R. Morris/DOC, 72tr: R. Morris/DOC, 72bl: DOC; 73bl: R. Colbourne/DOC, 73br: J.L. Kendrick/DOC; 74: A.K. Munn; 75–76: D. Merton/DOC; 77tl: M. Aviss/DOC, 77tr: D. Merton/DOC, 77cl: D. Merton/DOC, 77cr: D. Merton/DOC, 77bl: R. Morris/DOC, 77br: D. Merton/DOC; 78: D. Merton/DOC; 79tl: J.L. Kendrick/DOC, 79tr: R. Hay/DOC, 79bl: DOC, 79cr: DOC; 80: B. Robinson/DOC; 81: E.A. Humphreys/DOC; 82: DOC; 83: E.A. Humphreys/DOC; 84bl: D. Mudge/DOC, 84br: DOC; 85tr: K. Wells/DOC, 85bl: J. Hunt; 86t: S. Fordham/Naturepix, 86br: D. Eason/DOC; 87: J. Hunt; 88: S. Fordham/Naturepix; 89: R. Morris/DOC; 90: J. Maxwell/DOC; 91tr: P. Morrison/DOC, 91c: D. Eason/DOC, 91bl: D. Crouchley/DOC, 91br: D. Eason/DOC; 92: J. Hunt; 93tr: G. Climo/DOC, 93bl: DOC; 94–95: D. Veitch/DOC; 96–97: B. Barr/DOC; 98: G. Norman/DOC; 99: D. Veitch/DOC; 100: D. Stewart/Wingspan Birds of Prey Trust; 101–102: G. Loh/DOC; 103: R. Morris/DOC; 104: R. Colbourne/DOC; 105tr: D. Stewart/Wingspan Birds of Prey Trust, 105b: B.J. Harcourt; 106t: R. Morris/DOC. 106br: D. Merton/DOC; 107: D. Veitch/DOC; 108: DOC; 109b: R. Colbourne/DOC, 109cr: D. Veitch/DOC; 110t: R. Morris/DOC, 110r: M. Aviss/DOC; 112t: L.C. Hazley/DOC, 112b: D.G. Newman/DOC; 113tr: J. Gardenier/DOC, 113cr: J. Hunt; 114: DOC; 115: M. Aviss/DOC; 116: DOC; 117tr: B.W. Thomas/DOC, 117cr: D. Sanderson/DOC, 117bl: J. Nauta/Te Papa Tongarewa; 118: C.J.R. Robertson/DOC + J. Hunt; 119: A.E. Wright/DOC; 120tl: R. Morris/DOC, 120bl: D. Veitch/DOC, 120br: C.D. Roderick; 121t: R. Morris/DOC, 121b: N. Peat/DOC; 122: M.F. Soper/DOC; 123t: J. Hunt, 123b: A.E. Wright/DOC; 124: C.J.R. Robertson.

Index

42, the falcon 100–103, 105

A
albatross 5, 6, 118–123
amphibians 10, 47, 48, 49
Anderson, Richard 114
Andrews, Ivan 29
annelids 36
Aroha, the takahe 86, 87, 88
arthropods 36
Atiu, or Middle Mercury Island 81, 82, 83
Attenborough, David 16
Auckland Zoo 83

B
Barrett, Paul 83
bat 6, 11, 62–67
bat detector 63–65
bat fly 67
bellbird, see korimako
Ben Barr 95–98
Billing, Tony 75
black robin 31, 74–78
Black, Terry 61
Blue duck, see whio
Boundary Stream Reserve 55
Brown, Derek 45–48, 77
Buckingham, Rhys 51–54
Buller, Walter Lowry 99
Burwood Bush 22, 90–91
Buttons, the albatross 119–121

C
Campbell Island 5, 42, 122
Captive Breeding 25, 26, 28, 31, 91
Caskey, Dean 59
Catlins 42, 53
cat 6, 17, 23, 27, 31, 32, 41, 46, 53, 63, 73, 78, 81, 84, 96, 97, 99, 103, 105, 117, 122
cattle 27
Chalky Island, see Te Kakahu
Chatham Islands 75–78
Chatham Island warblers 76
chiroptologist 64
Clarkson, Jim 59
Clout, Dr Mick 18
Codfish Island, see Whenua Hou
Colbourne, Rogan 72
Colson, Mark 25
Cook Strait 45, 46, 52, 111, 113, 115
cow 6
cuckoo 73, 76, 79
Cuvier Island 97

D
deer 6, 93, 101
Delcourt, Alain 117
Dilks, Peter 79
dinosaur 9–11, 113
disease 6, 41, 47, 82, 95–97, 109
dodo 82
dog 6, 11, 15–16, 19–21, 41, 49, 70, 73, 81–82, 88, 102–3, 112, 122
Douglas, Charles 20, 69, 71

E
East Cape 82
Eglinton Valley 79
Egmont National Park 59, 60
Elkington, Simon 28
entemologist 83

F
Falconry 103
ferret 6, 20, 27, 31–33, 41, 70, 105
Fiordland 12, 15–18, 20, 33, 72, 88, 90, 93, 104, 108
Fraser, Marlia 102
frog 44–49

G
gecko 83–84, 117
giant eagle 13
giant weta 46, 84–85
global warming 41, 48
goat 6, 54, 66
Gondwana 10, 61, 66, 113
Grandma, the albatross 119, 121
Grant, Anna 70
Günther, Dr Albert 113

H
Hamilton's frog 45–49
harrier hawk, see kahu
Hauraki Gulf 17, 20, 87, 97
Hauturu, or Little Barrier Island 16, 17, 20, 97, 99
hedgehog 6, 27, 31, 33, 37, 81
Hen Island 57, 97
Henry, Richard (kakapo) 15
Henry, Richard (man) 20
herpetologist 46–47, 117
hihi 13, 94–99
hoiho 38–43, 122, 125
Hudson, Jeff 55
huia 57

I
insect 10, 11, 30, 36, 49, 56, 60, 66, 72, 76, 79, 104, 108, 109, 111
invertebrate 6, 11, 35, 37, 49, 57, 61, 72, 103, 104

J
Jensen, John 25
Jones, Grant 55

K
kahu 104
kaka 13, 97, 106–109
kakapo 14–23, 52, 66, 82, 109, 125
kakariki 97, 109
kaki, or black stilt 24–32, 41, 91
Kanavakoa, Lorna 114
Kapiti Island 7, 20, 54, 71–72, 87, 90, 93, 95, 97, 98, 109
karearea, or falcon 100–105, 125
Karori Wildlife Sanctuary 7, 57, 72
kawekaweau, or great gecko 117
Kawerau-a-Maki 92
Kawhitu, or Stanley Island 83, 116
kea 13, 106–109
Kendrick, John 52–54
King Country 54, 85
King, Sarah 55, 57
kiore 6, 97, 113
kiwi 20, 37, 68–73, 84, 125
kokako 46, 50–57, 73
korimako, or bellbird 79, 95–98

L
Lake Rotoiti mainland island 109
Lake Te Anau 89
Landcare Research 82
Laurasia 10
Little Barrier, see also Hauturu 16, 17, 54, 85, 97, 109
Little Mangere Island 75–76
Lloyd, Brian 64
Lyall, David 46

M
magpie 102
mainland island 7, 57, 85, 109
mammal 10, 11, 37, 66, 73, 81
Mahoenui 85
Mana Island 85, 90
Manganui-a-te-ao River 32–33

Mangere Island 75–78
Mapara Forest 54
Marlborough 17, 47, 70, 87, 103, 108, 113
Martin, Ross 70
Massey University 70, 102
Matiu Island 7, 113–114, 116
Maud Island, see Te Hoiere
McFadden, Ian 115
melanistic 31
Mercury Islands 83, 116
Merton, Don 16, 18–19, 22, 75, 79
mouse 6, 11, 37, 46, 83, 84
moa 8–13, 16, 69
mohoua, or yellowhead 79
Moorcroft, Greg 98
Motuara 70, 71
Mount Bruce National Wildlife Centre 16, 54
Mount Ruapehu 63
Mount Taranaki 33, 60, 61
Mrs Bones 25–26, 31
Murchison Mountains 88, 89

N
ngakeoke 34–37
Ngati Kuia 18
Northland 82, 97

O
Okarito 68, 70, 71–72
Old Blue, the black robin 75, 76, 77
Operation Nest Egg 70, 71
Orbell, Geoffrey 88
Otamatuna 55
Owen, Richard 93

P
Pangea 10
Pekapeka tou poto, or bat 62, 63
penguin, see hoiho
peripatus, see ngakeoke
pig 6, 61, 63, 66, 82
Pigeon Island 20
pipiwharauroa, or shining cuckoo 73, 79
Pitt Island 78
Pluto, the bat 64
Poaka or pied stilt 30, 31
Poor Knights Islands 115
possum 6, 17, 54, 60, 70, 81, 105, 109
powelliphanta 58–61
pukeko 73, 93

R
rabbit 6, 20, 27
Rangataua 63–65
ratite 11, 72

rat 6, 17, 20, 23, 27, 31, 32, 33, 37, 41, 54, 60, 61, 66, 69, 71, 79, 81, 84, 85, 96, 97, 105, 109, 113, 122
Raukumara 82
reptile 6, 10, 11, 47, 113, 115
Resolution Island 20
Richdale, Dr Lance 122
Rowi, or Okarito kiwi 69–72
Royal Forest and Bird Protection Society 36, 70
Ruataniwha 29, 31

S
saddleback, see tieke
Salmon, Guy 52
Sancha, Emily 26–29
sheep 6, 41, 75, 101, 108, 115
skink 83, 84, 114, 117
Smith, Hal 107, 126
snail 9, 10, 33, 58–61
Snider, Antoine 10
Somes Island, see Matiu
South East Island 76, 77, 78
Stephens Island, see Takapourewa
Stewart, Debbie 102
Stewart Island 17, 42, 51–53, 57, 72, 104
stitchbird, see hihi
stilt, see kaki or poaka
stoat 6, 17–18, 20, 23, 27, 31, 33, 41, 54, 60, 61, 69–71, 79, 81, 84, 91, 93, 105, 109, 122

T
Taiaroa Head 118–122
takahe 4, 22, 52, 86–91, 93, 117, 125
Takapourewa 45–48
Tamarapa, Koro 114
Tane, god of the forest 73, 79
Taranaki 32–33, 58–61
Taxonomy, the science of names 13
Te Anau 22, 89, 90
Te Atiawa 113
Te Hoiere, or Maud Island 16, 17, 18, 49, 87, 90, 93
Te Kakahu, or Chalky Island 18
Te Kuiti 85
Te Urewera National Park 54, 55
Thorpe, Rick 77
tieke, or saddleback 57
Tiritiri Matangi Island 7, 54, 57, 87, 88, 90, 92, 97, 125
tomtit 31, 76–77
Tongariro National Park 63
toroa, see albatross
toutouwai pango, or black robin 74, 75

tuatara 46, 47, 49, 82–84, 97, 110–117
tui 53, 73, 95–98
tusked weta 81–84
Twizel 25, 26, 28, 91

U
ultrasound 63

V
van Klink, Paul 71

W
Wairarapa 16, 54, 97, 125
walking worm 35–36
Walter, Barbara 87
Walter, Ray 92
Ward, Megan 55
weasel 6, 20, 33
Webb, Shirley 121
Wegener, Alfred 10
weka 93
Wellington 7, 57, 72, 113
weta, 9, 35, 37, 46, 76, 80–85, 97, 111, 114
Whatapuke Island 115
Whenua Hou, or Codfish Island 17, 18, 21
whio, or blue duck 32–33
Whitaker, Tony 82
whitehead 79
Wildlife Service 7, 16, 17, 18, 75, 76
Wingspan Birds of Prey Trust 102, 103
wood rose 67
worms 10, 30, 36, 69, 76
wren 11, 46, 73

Y
yellowhead, see mohoua
yellow-eyed penguin, see hoiho